Theological Education on Five Continents
Anabaptist Perspectives

Nancy R. Heisey and
Daniel S. Schipani, editors

Mennonite World Conference
Strasbourg, France
1997

MENNONITE WORLD CONFERENCE (MWC)

Mennonite, Brethren in Christ, and related churches form the Mennonite World Conference. MWC promotes solidarity and accountability between member churches by providing for communion, communication and cooperation. More than 80 conferences in some 50 nations are members or associate members. They appoint delegates to the general council which meets triennially and elects the executive committee. A global assembly convenes regularly; Assembly 13 met in Calcutta, India (January, 1997). MWC maintains a permanent secretariat currently located at 8 rue du Fossé des Treize, 67000 Strasbourg, France.

PRESENTATION

Larry Miller (France)
Executive Secretary
Mennonite World Conference

Seeing is believing, some say. But the most visible is not always the most significant. The Consultation on Theological Education on Five Continents was not the centerpiece of India 1997, MWC's thirteenth world assembly. Yet, from some points of view, it was one of the most important events in those first days of January.

What are the primary needs within the Mennonite and Brethren in Christ family today? Conversations with national leaders worldwide place two items at the top of the list: leadership training and identity formation. Who will lead us in the days ahead? And where will they lead us? For a variety of reasons, both the older churches (European, North American) and the younger ones (African, Asian, Central and South American) agree on this agenda. In this context, international reflection on theological education and transnational pooling of educational resources are not only timely but vital.

The shifting center in the global family increases the urgency of the endeavor. While more than half of Mennonites and Brethren in Christ now live in the South, resources—including theological training resources—are concentrated heavily in the North. Exchange and realignment are indispensable if we hope to remain only a few steps behind the movement of the Spirit across the face of the earth.

If that conviction led MWC to convene the Consultation on Theological Education on five Continents, it also prompted the MWC Executive Committee to approve the Consultation's "recommendations and projections" (cf. p. 131). Meeting in July 1997, these church leaders from five continents agreed that MWC would (1) make available Consultation materials, (2) encourage research and sharing, and (3) foster further dialogue and collaboration.

This book is the initial step towards meeting those objectives. May you be enriched by it and then contribute personally to their realization.

Occasional Papers

Theological Education on Five Continents is a Mennonite World Conference publication in cooperation with the Institute of Mennonite Studies. As such it will be part of the IMS *Occasional Papers* series.

Occasional Papers is a publication of the Institute of Mennonite Studies and authorized by the Council of Mennonite Seminaries. The three sponsoring seminaries are Eastern Mennonite Seminary (Harrisonburg, VA), Associated Mennonite Biblical Seminary (Elkhart, IN), and the Mennonite Brethren Biblical Seminary (Fresno, CA). The Institute of Mennonite Studies is the research agency of the Associated Mennonite Biblical Seminary.

Occasional Papers is released without any prescribed calendar schedule. The purpose of the Papers is to make various types of essays available to foster dialogue in biblical, theological and practical ministry areas and to invite critical counsel from within the Mennonite theological community. While most essays will be in finished form, some may also be in a more germinal stage—released especially for purposes of testing and receiving critical feedback. In accepting papers for publication, priority will be given to authors from the CMS institutions, the college Bible faculties in the Council of Mennonite Colleges, the associate membership of the Institute of Mennonite Studies, and students and degree alumni of the three seminaries.

Because of limited circulation of the Occasional Papers, authors are free to use their material in other scholarly settings, either for oral presentation at scholarly meetings or for publication in journals with broader circulation and more official publication policies.

Copyright 1997 for this volume by Mennonite World Conference, 8, rue du Fossé des Treize, 67000 Strasbourg, France. Tel (33) 3-88-15-27-50. Fax (33) 3-88-15-27-51. No part of this publication may be reproduced, stored in a retrieval system, or transmitted in any form or by any means, electronic, mechanical, photocopying, or otherwise, without the prior permission of the copyright owner.

Grateful acknowledgement to the Mennonite Board of Education for a Peoplehood Education grant to print this English version; to Ruth Liechty - Composition; Mary E. Klassen - Art; Phyllis Horst Nofziger - Secretarial assistance; Evangel Press - Printing.

ISBN 0-936273-27-5
Printed in the USA

Contents

Presentation, Larry Miller (France) iii
Introduction..1

Foundations and Framework

1. *The Church and Its Theological Education: A Vision* 5
   Daniel S. Schipani (Argentina/USA)

The Task and the Challenges of Theological Education

2. *Congregational Theological Education: Congregational Education*, Leonor de Méndez (Guatemala)......................39
   Responses:
      Cathy Mputo (Congo) 44
      Mikha Joedhiswara (Indonesia) 47
      Ineke Reinhold-Scheuermann (The Netherlands) 53
      Heidi Regier Kreider (USA) 55

3. *Non-Formal Theological Education: The Meserete Kristos Church Experience*, Bedru Hussein (Ethiopia) 57
   Responses:
      Wendy Binks (India)..84
      José Gallardo (Spain) 88
      John Powell (USA) 93
      Helen Dueck (Canada/Bolivia) 99

4. *Formal Theological Education: The Centre and the Boundaries*, Lydia Harder (Canada)............................103
   Responses:
      Bruce Khumalo (Zimbabwe).......................................113
      Jaime Prieto (Costa Rica)..116
      V.K. Rufus (India)..121
      Bernhard Ott (Switzerland) 123

Conclusion...127

Consultation Participants...132
Institutions and Programs 134

INTRODUCTION

The Consultation on Theological Education on Five Continents (CTEFC) grew out of an interest by the Institute of Mennonite Studies,[1] and a desire expressed by the General Council of Mennonite World Conference (MWC), to enhance communication among theological educators in MWC member conferences and to pursue better understandings of the distinctiveness of Anabaptist theological education. Convened by the MWC, the gathering was intended for persons involved in theological education at many levels of congregational, formal, and non-formal theological education in the global Mennonite and Brethren in Christ family of faith. The three stated goals were to promote: (1) reflection on the broad vision of how theological education strengthens and renews Anabaptist churches for their worship, community, and mission; (2) exchange from different experiences of the practical means of carrying out theological education tasks; and (3) opportunities to build networks for continuing interchange of educational resources.

The Consultation took place on January 1 and 2 at Morningstar College, a Roman Catholic seminary located in Barrackpore (West Bengal), India, a few days before the MWC Assembly in Calcutta. Despite pre-meeting communication difficulties, the limitations of volunteer staff, and severe restrictions on funding, about 50 people from more than 20 countries participated in this event. They represented a variety of regions, cultures and church realities within Africa, Asia, Europe, Latin America, and North America.[2]

---

[1] The Institute of Mennonite Studies (IMS) is an integral part of the Associated Mennonite Biblical Seminary located in Elkhart (Indiana), United States of America. The overall purpose of the Institute is "to provide facilities for, to promote, and to administer a program of study in fields of direct interest to the faith, life, work and witness of the Mennonites in the modern world as well as in the past...The Institute shall also seek to cultivate such inter-Mennonite and related denominational relationships as may facilitate cooperative studies on specific projects which serve the broader Anabaptist-Mennonite and related constituencies and be supportive of their common goals." (from the IMS charter).

[2] Participants who arrived early joined in an informal New Year's Eve service where each one shared the gift of a favorite Scripture with

The structure and content of this book closely reflect the program design of the Consultation. Four plenary working sessions provided the framework for the meeting, beginning with a presentation and discussion of a vision of the church and its theological education; the second, third, and fourth sessions consisted of presentations and responses pertaining to congregational, non-formal and formal theological education, respectively. The material presented in each case constitutes the body of the volume in chapters 1 through 4.

Representatives of the five continents met in caucuses on the first afternoon. On the second afternoon, interest groups discussed theological education issues concerning women, pastoral formation, mission, working with children and youth, and administration. The whole group met in a final session to reflect on the event and to list ongoing issues and needs. The conclusion of this book includes a summary of discussion highlights, a reference to issues raised which call for further consideration, and recommendations and projections.

---

another member of the group. The Consultation convened formally on New Year's morning. Worship was characterized by its representation of the many gifts of the worldwide Mennonite and Brethren in Christ fellowship, marked especially by music—16th century German hymns, African American gospel songs, and Telegu choruses. In all the sessions, participants struggled with the realities of the multi-lingual nature of the group and a meeting room with poor acoustics, but were blessed by the patient labors of several volunteer interpreters. Nancy R. Heisey was the Secretary and main organizer of the Consultation, and Daniel S. Schipani was the appointed Consultant.

Foundations and Framework

We consider theological education as a special dimension of the church's larger teaching ministry, and also as a special setting and process for the church's theological task. Our fundamental common assumption is that **we engage in theological education for the sake of the church in the world in the light of God's reign.**

The church is called to live, to share and to sponsor trinitarian faith in everyday life animated by the presence of God. Normally, church life and ministry take place in three essential arenas: worship, community, and mission. These are the three necessary, inseparable, and interrelated dimensions that functionally define the church's reason for being.

Within an Anabaptist framework, *theological education…*

…will be designed in terms of a church-based model. Our biblical and theological foundations point us toward such a model focused on the church's identity, nature, and purpose;

…will contribute to the grounding, education for, and evaluation of the Christian ministry of pastors, teachers and other leaders, in the congregation and beyond. This ministry is designed to equip the entire community for worship, community and mission;

…will include three interrelated contexts and agendas: the context and agenda of the church as well as its history and traditions; the socio-cultural context and agenda of our world, both narrowly and broadly; and the context of God's commonwealth of freedom, justice and peace, and God's agenda revealed in Word and Spirit;

…will have a "hermeneutical circulation"—the movement between reflection and action— as both the key to how we do theological education and the centerpiece of what we teach and learn.

1

The Church and Its Theological Education: A Vision
Daniel S. Schipani (Argentina/USA)

The statement of purpose of the Consultation included the goal of promoting reflection on how theological education (TE) strengthens and renews Anabaptist churches for their life of worship, community, and mission. Implicit in that goal is a fundamental assumption that can be stated as the answer to the question, "Why do we do TE?": *We engage in TE for the sake of the church in the world in the light of God's reign*. This essay is meant to contribute to that reflection on the place and function of TE in the face of the challenges and opportunities our churches encounter in diverse social and cultural contexts as well as on the global scene. The following introductory remarks may be helpful before we propose a way to view the church and to design its TE.

We consider TE as a special dimension of the church's larger teaching ministry,[1] and also as a special setting and process for the church's theological task[2]. TE, sometimes also called "Bible

---

[1] The reference to the larger teaching ministry alludes to all the divers ways in which the work of educating for the life of the Christian faith is carried out. It thus includes different kinds of activities, programs, modes, and settings—formal and informal—such as teaching through preaching, Sunday school and other classes, Bible study courses, mentoring, spiritual direction, catechism, various forms of leadership and ministry training, and so on. TE has a special place and function within this comprehensive field of church education, including the task of supporting and enhancing the teachings of the church and educating the church's teachers.

[2] We view theology as closely connected to the teaching ministry of the church; in fact, as a disciplined body of knowledge and way of thinking, theology grows out of and informs that ministry. As a disciplined body of knowledge, theology includes the study and appropriation of the church's normative traditions, the criteria for making judgments about faithful beliefs and practices, and the language in which the church best articulates its message. As a disciplined way of thinking, theology seeks to bring coherence, consistency, insight, and intellectual rigor to both the

training" or "biblical education,"³ is concerned with the formation and transformation of the faith community—"strengthening and

---

critical and constructive tasks of the church's teaching ministry. Taken together, the responsibilities of the church's teaching and theological ministry are at least threefold, each having critical and constructive tasks. Those responsibilities include: (a) passing on traditions which have proven to be carriers of faithful witness to God's reign; (b) providing guidance to help bodies of believers in diverse cultural settings make wise judgments about normative Christian beliefs and practices; and (c) articulating the church's message in ways that nurture Christian life and faith in the contemporary world. From, *Ministerial Formation and Theological Education in Mennonite Perspective* (statement of philosophy of education of the Associated Mennonite Biblical Seminary, Elkhart, IN, USA; adopted 1992), pp. 5-6.

³Our preference is to keep using the term "theological education" while assuming that TE is necessarily *biblical* education. Within an Anabaptist framework and perspective we hold certain normative convictions concerning the Bible: it is God's Word written and its authority has its ultimate source in God; it must be interpreted, understood and applied to our life and ministry in the light of Jesus Christ as we are led by the Holy Spirit in the church. Therefore, in a fundamental sense all forms of church education must actually be considered and carried out as "*biblical education*". There are at least four reasons for making such a proposal: a) the Bible is the primary and indispensable text for the church, especially in terms of its substantive content culminating in the witness to the life, ministry and saving work of Jesus Christ; (b) the biblical material supplies key, essential anthropological, epistemological and ethical foundations for education, such as its manifold insights regarding ways of being, knowing and loving; (c) in addition to its direct pertinence and reference (e.g. the study of Bible passages and books as such), biblical material must critically and constructively inform whatever else we do and deal with in TE (e.g. peace studies, leadership training, justice making, pastoral care and counseling, etc.); (d) TE necessitates an ongoing, biblically grounded spirituality on the part of teachers and learners, to be nurtured by prayerful, devotional encounters with the Bible.

A twofold qualifying note might also be in order here. While affirming the unique, indispensable and foundational place and role of Scripture in the teaching ministry, including TE, we recognize that the study of the Bible is not an end in itself—it must happen for the sake of growth in the love of God and neighbor; further, the ultimate foundation for our life is not the Bible but Jesus Christ (I Cor.3:11).

renewing", in the language of the CTEFC purpose statement—and with the enablement and equipment for ministry in particular. At the risk of oversimplifying, then, TE can be understood primarily, though certainly not exclusively, as "*education for apostleship*".[4]

The first part of this paper—"Visioning the Church"—is a discussion of the church's identity, character and reason for being in light of trinitarian foundations[5]. It is included here because our own teaching ministry and theological reflection have been significantly illumined by keeping such an ecclesiological base in focus.[6] The second part—"Shaping Theological Education"— suggests a number of implications that can be drawn from such a view of the church.

---

[4]By this phrase—suggested by Erland Waltner, former president of the Mennonite Biblical Seminary in Elkhart, IN., USA—we mean the training of men and women to be faithful and competent servants of Jesus Christ, that is, the formation of ministering persons, including leadership ministries—e.g. pastors—as well as other ministries. Thus viewed, TE obviously builds on and supplements the fundamental and lifelong "education for *discipleship*," or education for growth in the life of the Christian faith.

[5]Our Anabaptist-Mennonite tradition for the most part has affirmed a trinitarian orthodoxy in its doctrine of God. It can be argued that a distinctive quality of such an affirmation has been a concern not so much for doctrinal orthodoxy in its own right as for the ecclesiological and therefore ethical function of the Christian doctrine of the Triune God. See A. James Reimer, "God (Trinity), Doctrine of", *The Mennonite Encyclopedia*, vol. V, Cornelius J. Dyck & Denis D. Martin, eds. (Scottdale/Waterloo: Herald Press, 1990) pp. 342-348.

[6]Reflection on this topic of trinitarian foundations for the church's teaching ministry began for us in the context of an inter-Mennonite project—"Future Models of Congregational Education"—in the late 80's. Earlier versions of the following discussion appear in Daniel S. Schipani, "Crezcamos en todo...en Cristo", Fraternidad Teológica Latinoamericana, *Misión en el camino: ensayos en homenaje a Orlando E. Costas* (Florida: FTL, 1992) pp. 115-128, and Schipani et. al., *Comunicación con la juventud: Diseño para una nueva pastoral* (San Juan: Seminario Evangélico de Puerto Rico, 1994), chapters 2, 3.

VISIONING THE CHURCH

The life and destiny of the church can be viewed in terms of the church's perception and understanding of itself: its identity, nature and ministry, and its reason for being in the midst of world and history. The church sees itself as called to be God's alternative community in the context of the historical situation, like a "city on a hill" (Mt 5:14). Instructed by the declaration found in the letter to the Ephesians concerning the "fullness of God" and "the full stature of Christ" (3:19, 4:13), the church audaciously assumes that, in terms of divine expectations, it is called to become God's project for the world, God's dream in the process of being realized. The church, inspired and guided by the Holy Spirit (Jn 20:21-22), is to carry on Jesus' own ministry. In other words, the church views itself as that section of humanity in which Christ is actually taking form.[7]

Witnessing to God's coming reign is thus the church's primary agenda: to be a sign of divine life and love and to demonstrate and foster the freedom, justice and peace that God wills for all. The church is then viewed not only in terms of a historical process of foundation and pilgrimage, but primarily as God's creation—the fruit of divine grace and a special expression of divine love.[8] Therefore, a certain fundamental correlation can be

---

[7]Such a bold perception and declaration is found in theologians who do not necessarily represent a "sectarian" view of the church, such as Dietrich Bonhoeffer (see for instance, *Ethics*, trans. Neville Horton Smith, 6th. ed. [New York: Macmillan, 1955], p. 83).

[8]The systematic theological study of the church (ecclesiology) can start with the "foundation" of the Church by Jesus Christ or, at least, with the focus on the historical continuity linking Jesus' life and ministry, his death and resurrection, with Pentecost and the historical beginnings of early Christian faith communities. Another starting place, not necessarily in contradiction with the historical one, to be sure, is the theological claim of the church's divine origin in the saving grace and will of God. Blending both views is the normative conviction that, like Jesus Christ himself, the church must be seen as the sacrament of God's saving will and of God's very own self. For a clear presentation of this topic, see Robert Kress, *The Church: Communion, Sacrament, Communication* (New York: Paulist, 1985), Introduction, pp. 30 ff. From the perspective of practical

established between our views of God and our ways of understanding the church.⁹ And since Christian faith imagines the Divine as the triune God—the eternal communion of Father, Son, and Holy Spirit—it follows that the church (whether the local faith community or congregation, or the "universal" church) is meant to partake somehow of God's trinitarian nature and is called to be a sacrament of the Trinity.¹⁰

Biblical images and metaphors for the church are manifold and multifaceted. In fact, rather than limiting themselves to a few images organized in some systematic fashion, New Testament writers opted for the richness of varied images to describe the

---

church's life and ministry—different implications and ramifications can be drawn from the "historical" and the "theological" ecclesiological starting points. In the former case, practical theologians will focus for instance on the narratives of the book of Acts (especially 2: 42, 44-47) and discuss activities of ecclesial ministry identified as *kerygma, didache, leiturgia, koinonia,* and *diakonia* as being on the same plane, as it were; the best illustration of this is Maria Harris' excellent book, *Fashion Me a People: Curriculum in the Church* (Louisville: W/JKP, 1989). In the case of the "theological" starting point, which is represented in this essay, the trinitarian base points instead to what we call the church's threefold reason for being—*worship, community,* and *mission.* Ministry (whatever the modes, forms, and settings) then is viewed primarily at the service of such a threefold reason for being, that is, as the multifaceted art and task of enabling for worship, equipping for community, and empowering for mission. Further, as we will demonstrate in the second part of this paper, such a trinitarian base also suggests that ministry can be further defined as sponsoring human emergence in the light of Jesus Christ.

⁹There is of course a noble tradition of explicitly connecting the Trinity with the church going back at least to Tertullian (160? - 225?) and to Cyprian (c 205 - 258).

¹⁰The language of the church as sacrament and icon of the Trinity has been re-appropriated in a fresh way among Roman Catholics after Vatican II (see *Lumen Gentium,* no. 4) and it has also been proposed in the framework of ecumenical conversations; see, Bruno Forte, *The Church: Icon of the Trinity,* trans. Robert Paolucci (Boston: St. Paul Books, 1991). We understand the notion of the church as sacrament in the threefold sense of *symbol, icon* or *image* (that represents God's life and will), *sign* (which points to God's presence and activity) and *agent* (as instrument of God's grace and salvation). We trust that such understanding is consistently reflected in this chapter.

complex reality of the church.[11] At the same time, the early Christian community realized that its identity was fundamentally grounded in the one God, one Lord, and one Spirit (I Cor 12:4-6, Eph 4:4-6). Thus a correlation was early established between trinitarian notions regarding God's being/work and the nature/ministry of the church: the life of the transcendent Creator, historic Redeemer, and immanent Spirit is reflected in the historical reality of the church. In the next section we will discuss briefly the three main figures of speech associated with the church's identity and character; we will then focus on the actual ecclesial praxis as expression of its threefold reason for being.

The Church's Threefold Identity and Character:
People of God, Body of Christ, Temple of the Spirit

How the church partakes of and reflects God's trinitarian life and activity in the world is especially illuminated in the three biblical images of (*covenant*) *people of God, body of Christ*, and *temple* (or *dwelling*) *of the Spirit*. These are the three symbols traditionally highlighted in reference to the trinitarian character of the church; the three must be considered together and as closely interrelated.

---

[11]In his landmark study, *Images of the Church in the New Testament* (Philadelphia: Westminster, 1960), Paul Minear talks about more than eighty separate analogies and ninety-six major and minor images. Nevertheless, he finds that there is a certain unity in all that diversity for "as a matter of fact, each major image points toward a perception of the character of the church that agrees, to an amazing degree, with the perceptions produced by other images" (p. 26). Each of those images seem to disclose a particular perception of the church which arose out of the earliest Christian experience of the faith community. Minear also observes that the multiple images were used descriptively as forms of self-recognition adapted by a community whose sense of uniqueness stemmed from the fact that its overall orientation was always centered beyond itself in the activity of Father, Son, and Holy Spirit. See also, Harold S. Bender, *These Are My People* (Scottdale: Herald Press, 1962), especially chapters 1, 2, 3; and John Driver, *Images of the Church in Mission* (Scottdale: Herald Press, 1997).

People of God. This first image underscores that the church belongs to God, both in its origin and in its history; this symbol solidly grounds the church in the faith of Israel and evokes godliness as a people. Even sin and fallenness cannot destroy such godliness (Hos 2:24-25). As God's chosen possession (Deut 7:6), the church affirms its creation, sustenance and goal in God. In the New Testament, this motif is applied afresh to the "new" people of God whose character and destiny are now explicitly connected to Jesus Christ. "People of God" includes the non-Jewish, pagan folks also reconciled to God through the Christ (Rom 9:25). The divinely granted and established sense of identity and dignity—as "a chosen race, a royal priesthood, a holy nation, God's own people"—is especially authenticated in the midst of difficult historical circumstances (I Pet 2:4-10).

As covenant people, the church is called to live in reverent and loyal communion with God (or "to walk humbly with God," Mic 6:8) in light of the divine will expressed in the imperatives, promises and directions of the politics of God. *Worship* is, therefore, the primary arena of the church's life and ministry in which covenant peoplehood is enacted and the reign of God is duly acknowledged and celebrated. The call to remain in covenant requires the church to live in tune with God's purpose and activity in history and thus to grow in fidelity and maturity according to God's criteria for true *faithfulness*.[12] Hence, a key challenge for the

---

[12]It can be argued that the church is expected to grow wholistically and consistently with its trinitarian nature. That is precisely the constructive A Wholistic Concept of Church proposal stated insightfully by Orlando E. Costas in, "Growth," Wilbert R. Shenk, ed. *Exploring Church Growth* (Grand Rapids: Eerdmans, 1983) pp. 95-107. Costas discusses theologically identifiable qualities of authentic ecclesial emergence articulated in terms of *faithfulness, spirituality,* and *incarnation*; in his proposal, these qualities become necessary theological criteria for assessing different dimensions of church and faith growth. We have deliberately inverted the connection that Costas establishes between body of Christ and dwelling or fellowship of the Spirit, on the one hand, and incarnation and spirituality, on the other; the reason is that we prefer to stress the dialectical tension suggested by the notions of Christ's body growing in spirituality, and the dwelling of the Spirit growing in incarnation.

church is to discern whether its life and work truthfully correspond to the politics of God and to God's *vision* for life and for the world.

Body of Christ. This second image is derived from the Pauline focus on the church as a living organism which incarnates the life and love of Christ and shares that life communally and in unity. This metaphor brightly highlights both the communion of the church's members with one another (as presented in Romans and I Corinthians) as well as their communion with Christ as the head (as indicated in Colossians and Ephesians).[13] Such teaching can be theologically juxtaposed with the language of John's gospel. In Jesus' designation of himself as the true vine in chapter 15, and also in his promise of the gift of the Spirit of truth, John makes colorfully explicit that the source of this communion is the Father, God the Creator and vinegrower, and that Jesus—the Word made flesh—is the actual locus of this deeply spiritual communion among fruitful branches which abide firmly in the vine.

Constituted of many members—each a unique expression of divine life and love—the church as Christ's body in the world is called to grow in communion and holiness (or, "to love kindly," Mic 6:8), that is, in authentic *spirituality*. In that light, the church seeks to grow to maturity as a rich garden of relationships, where complementary gifts and functions are exercised through the empowerment of the Holy Spirit. *Community* life is thus the privileged arena in which the church enacts its being Christ's spiritual body. A key challenge for the ecclesial community, therefore, is to discern whether its actual experience and ministry correspond to the character or *virtue* of Jesus Christ and to his ethic of divine, compassionate love.

---

[13]As Kress reminds us, the earlier Pauline epistles are primarily concerned with the local church as the body of Christ, that is, one *body* from many different members: the faith community is thus viewed as a charismatic organism; the later epistles focus more on the "universal" church and the emphasis is on the communion of the body with its head, who is also Christ. There is no contradiction between these two emphases. And, citing Heinrich Schleier, "Only when the church is understood as both the charismatic organism and the cosmos of Christ is the ecclesiological description of the church as body of Christ fully present." *The Church: Communion, Sacrament, Communication*, p. 69.

Temple of the Spirit. This third image evokes the conviction and the hope that the church is also "being built together spiritually into a dwelling place for God" (Eph 2:22) in the midst of history. Accordingly, the church must be considered not only as people of God and as the body of Christ but also (communally and personally) as temple of the Holy Spirit (I Cor 3:16-17, 6:19). Again, points of significant theological continuity between various New Testament strands can be highlighted: for instance, the notion of Jesus' body as temple found in John's Gospel (2:19-22), Jesus' teaching that delocalizes the actual temple as the place reserved for God's true presence and worship (Jn 4:21-24), and the Acts narrative of Pentecost when the Spirit of God is generously poured on the church. As graced humanity, the church thus becomes, like Jesus Christ, a special sacrament of universal salvation and a dwelling place for God, a "temple" where God can be encountered and worshipped,[14] where a new community of humanity is being formed and participation in God's mission in the world is sought and sponsored.

The temple image suggests that the church is a dynamic, discerning, and gifted expression of God's grace and power in the world and for the sake of the world. The church is called to become a company of people who are a truthful sign of the presence, the purposes and the activity of God through their own socio-historical presence (as "salt" and "light") and through word and deed they responsibly and timely express divine love. As special dwelling place of the Spirit, the church seeks "to do justice" (Mic 6:8) as it grows in apostolicity, unity, and *incarnation. Mission* is thus the principal arena for the church to enact "temple of the Holy Spirit" in the midst of history. A key challenge for the church is, therefore, to discern whether its witness is in tune with God's will and grace and whether it carries out in hope the *vocation* of the Spirit in this world.

Together, then, these three images illuminate the church's identity and character as a reflection of God's own nature and activity as Creator, Redeemer, and Life-Giver. Such an ecclesiological restatement suggests a way of understanding

---

[14]Ibid., pp. 70-71.

ecclesial life and ministry, broadly viewed, by pointing to the church's threefold reason for being. This theme is considered in the next section with further implications and ramifications of our discussion so far.

The Church's Threefold Reason for Being: Worship, Community, Mission

The church is called to live, to share and to sponsor trinitarian faith in everyday praxis animated by the life of God. Normally—in a modest and imperfect manner, to be sure—ecclesial life and ministry take place in the context of three essential arenas: worship, community, and mission. These are the three necessary, inseparable, and interrelated dimensions that functionally define the church's "ecclesiality", its very reason for being. To state it in simplified and familiar terms: in worship we attend primarily to our life with God, in community to our life with one another, and in mission to our life in the wider world. In other words, an implicit correlation with the great commandment and its threefold love of God, and love of the neighbor as ourselves (Mk 12:28-34) is also assumed and intended here: worship, community, and mission are the arenas in which the life and ministry of the church are expected to unfold as especial, concrete, and contextualized manifestations of such three-dimensional love.[15]

As argued before, the church is at the same time people of God, body of Christ, and temple of the Spirit; analogously, and as a visible expression of the mystery of the Trinity, the church must be seen *perichoretically*.[16] In other words, worship, community, and

---

[15] In light of this understanding, then, a number of implications follow; for instance, that any adequate statement of identity and purpose articulated and made public by a given congregation or faith community will have to include explicit references to these three arenas and dimensions. Other ramifications will be indicated below.

[16] The term *perichoresis* means mutual indwelling or interpenetration and refers to the understanding of both the Trinity and Christology. There is a long tradition of thus visualizing and describing the inner relation among the persons of the Godhead going back to the Cappadocian Fathers (late 4th century) and John of Damascus (c. 675 - c. 749). The idea is that the divine modes of being mutually condition and permeate one another so completely that one is always in the other two.

mission, are not three parts or departments of the church, but the one church becoming and growing, and being renewed in those three specific manifestations of its historical expression. Authentic ecclesial communion and the unity of the church consist in a kind of "perichoresis" among all the faithful; the church becomes a figure of the Trinity, making it palpable to humankind, to the extent that it achieves such an interpenetration.[17]

It is readily apparent that the three dimensions cannot be neatly separated either in practice or in theory. Thus, when the congregation worships God together, the faithful can also experience the support and love of the community as well as the call to serve the world as representatives of Christ in the power of the Spirit. As they go about their task of peacemaking and service in the world, they carry with them the presence of the living God they worship, together with the marks of the faith community to which they belong. And when believers gather and relate to each other within the body which is the church, they may also pray and worship and anticipate their faithful witness beyond the church family. Further, it is also apparent that in "healthy" congregations the three arenas of life and ministry are developed and renewed simultaneously: a vital worship life creates a loving community and strengthens the church for its mission in the larger society; and responsible, pertinent ministry in the world calls people to disciplined worship and to a recognition of the need for strong community as well. For the purpose of further explication, the three dimensions can be examined briefly as discrete axes of experience, relationships, and action.

Some twentieth century theologians, such as Leonardo Boff, also use the notion metaphorically in referring to the nature of the church.

[17]Leonardo Boff, *Trinity and Society*, trans. Paul Burns (Maryknoll: Orbis, 1988) pp. 106-107. In that very short section on the ecclesial symbolism of the Trinity, Boff refers to the unity of the church being built around the axes of faith, worship, and organization for inner cohesion, mutual life and mission: "gathering to proclaim and deepen its faith; coming together to celebrate the presence of the *magnalia Dei* in history past and present; organized for the harmonious building of its own body, so that it can be of service to others, particularly the poor and those who have not heard its message." (Ibid.)

Worship. *The church exists first of all for the sake of worship, that is, for the acknowledgement and celebration of the reign of God.* In its life of worship (which is more than cultic experience on special days and times, to be sure), the church deliberately enters into God's presence and opens itself to the source of its being via scripture, prayer, ritual, proclamation, offering, music, silence, the arts, and so on. Persons are shaped and formed into a faithful covenant community by the story of God's acts in human history, their experience of divine love and power in the present, and their hope for the future fulfillment of God's reign; the deeply political significance of worship is thus underscored in the tradition of biblical faith. Certain specific practices and disciplines[18] must be highlighted as constitutive of worship: praising God, giving thanks in the face of God's creative,

---

[18]The term "practices" here and in the next section refers to those ongoing shared activities of the church that partly define it and partly fashion it as a faith community. The word "disciplines", alludes to those very practices in the sense of disciplined practices and highlights the deliberate, intentional, and focused nature of the church's practices. We want to emphasize the need for this understanding, which undergirds our view of ministry as redefined below, because of the peculiar character of the practices of the church: they are *historical, communal, difficult* (in the sense that they require the integration of knowledge and skill with appropriate attitude and perspective), and—at least partly—*countercultural*. On this point see Craig Dykstra, "No Longer Strangers: The Church and Its Educational Ministry," *Princeton Seminary Bulletin*, VI:3, (1985): 193-200. It is assumed, of course, that practices and disciplines are necessary and essential for the nurturing of faith and growth in the life of Christian faith or discipleship. This is the case not because they are viewed as bringing about, effecting or causing faith and the growth in faith; rather, as clearly put in a recent Presbyterian Church (USA) document, "...engagement in them puts us in a position where we may recognize and participate in the work of God's grace in the world. This is precisely what we do when we 'make diligent use of the means of grace.' By active participation in practices that are central to the historical life of the community of faith, we place ourselves in the kind of situation in which we know God accomplishes the work of grace." *Growing in the Life of Christian Faith* (Louisville: Theology and Worship Ministry Unit, Presbyterian Church [USA], 1989, 1991), p. 27.

liberating, and sustaining-renewing work; hearing the Word preached, confessing and repenting, and receiving the sacraments.

Trinitarian faith and life is thus expressed, shaped, and nurtured especially (though certainly not exclusively) in terms of the formation and growth of *vision*.[19] The connection between worship and vision is suggested in numerous biblical accounts, perhaps most paradigmatically in the story of Isaiah's call (Isa 6:1-8). This story's three movements reveal something which is essential in worship: 1) the prophet's eyes are opened to "see" God; 2) his eyes are opened to see himself (as he is in God's sight); 3) his eyes are further opened to see God's vision of the world. In short, worship and growth in vision are connected in that worship is a privileged place and occasion to receive revelation and thus to have our imagination transformed. Craig Dykstra says it well: "We get ourselves into a condition in which our imagination may be transformed so that we can come to see, think, feel, value, and act as reformed selves...In worship our disciplines take on liturgical form...When we come to worship, we come to put ourselves in a position to receive revelation...we see and sense who it is we are to be and how it is we are to move in order to become. Worship is an enactment of the core dynamics of the Christian life. This is why worship is the church's central and focusing activity. It is paradigmatic for all the rest of the Christian life."[20]

In sum, through participation in the various forms and settings of worship the church is confirmed as being indeed God's covenant people and as committed to faithful participation in the politics of God. Thus understood and lived out, worship sustains and inspires both life in community and the mission of the church

---

[19] A fuller explanation and discussion of what is meant here by *vision* (as well as *virtue* and *vocation*) appears in our essay, "The Purpose of Ministry: Human Emergence in the Light of Jesus Christ;" it is to be included in a book on pastoral theology.

[20] In Craig Dykstra, *Vision and Character: A Christian Educator's Alternative to Kohlberg* (New York: Paulist Press, 1981), pp 105-106. Another practical theologian, John H. Westerhoff, also helpfully underscores the *authorizing* function of worship (in the sense of its becoming the source of authority for faith and life by uniquely revealing God's truth); in *Living the Faith Community: The Church that Makes a Difference* (Minneapolis: Winston, 1985), chaps. 4, 5.

in the world. In turn, the church's life of worship is simultaneously enriched and supported by the experience and the practices of community and mission.

Community. *The church also exists to become community, that is, to embody the reign of God historically and socially in its own midst.* In its life of community, then, the church concretely participates in the family of God and the body of Christ. Persons can thus be nourished by experiences, relationships, and actions which form and transform them into Christlikeness in divers formal and informal processes and settings. Practices and disciplines constitutive of community would include these: persons learn to welcome, accept and listen to one another; they share with each other the story of the Christian faith as well as their own stories; they confess their sins, forgive one another and participate in reconciliation; they resist destructive powers, patterns and activities which destroy communion; they receive and give counsel and encourage and admonish one another; they engage in mutual gift discernment and affirmation; they learn from, care for and suffer for one another. These practices and disciplines are indicators of the deeply spiritual reality of *koinonia* to which the church is invited and for which it is empowered by God's Spirit. A pervasive formation and transformation process takes place as the church fulfills its social task of becoming a community of character (and of truly Christian characters). To put it in Stanley Hauerwas' terms, the primary and "the most important social task of Christians is to be nothing less than a community capable of forming people with virtues sufficient to witness to God's truth in the world...to become a polity that has the character necessary to survive as a truthful society."[21]

---

[21]Stanley Hauerwas, *A Community of Character: Toward a Constructive Social Ethic* (Notre Dame: Univ. of Notre Dame Press, 1981), p. 3; see esp. chapters 6, 7. Hauerwas advocates for the church to regain, in his words, "an appropriate sense of separateness from the larger society." Although we agree with much of his thought, we hold a more dynamic and dialectic view of the interface between church and society. For his part, Westerhoff—building on the contributions of Hauerwas and Walter Brueggemann—incisively articulates the church's challenge to sustain and nurture a countercultural consciousness in the world and to provide a

In sum, through participation in community, the church, corporately as well as individually, reflects the moral character of Jesus Christ and challenges persons to grow in authentic communion and spirituality. Trinitarian faith and life is therefore expressed, shaped and nurtured especially (but certainly not exclusively) in terms of formation and growth in *virtue*.[22] Thus understood and lived out, the life of the faith community encourages and strengthens both worship and mission. In turn, the life of the faith community is simultaneously sustained and enhanced by the church's experience and practices of worship and mission.

Mission. *The church also exists to be in mission, that is, to participate in the manifestations of the reign of God in the midst of history, and to witness by means of presence, word and deed.* In its mission, the church responds to the call to become a partner in God's graceful creating, liberating, and renewing activity in the world; it is present especially in the midst of human alienation, suffering and lostness, in the pain and destiny of all creation. Again, a number of practices and disciplines constitutive of mission illustrate the church's participation in society as Christ's representative: awareness and understanding of the context in which it lives; evangelistic, hopeful proclamation, and prophetic denunciation; multidimensional service for the sake of freedom, peace and justice; hospitality and care for strangers; stewardship and care of the nonhuman environment, etc. The church also seeks to discern and test the spirits of the times alongside the movement of God's Spirit in history. As the fellowship and temple of the Spirit, it receives spiritual gifts, discerns congregational and

---

witness to that consciousness by becoming an alternative community; *Living the Faith Community*, chap. 6.

[22]It is possible to identify specific ways in which the church is formative of character or virtue through historical drama, convictions and ways of seeing, stories, language, image, symbols and rituals, and forms of actions in common. See Dykstra, *Vision and Character,* pp. 55 ff.; also, "The Formative Power of Congregations," *Religious Education* 82 (1987): 530-546. See also Harry Huebner, "A Community of Virtues," Harry Huebner & David Schroeder, eds., *Church as Parable: Whatever Happened to Ethics* (Winnipeg: CMBC Publications, 1993), pp. 171-195.

personal direction, makes responsible ethical choices, and commits itself to loving ministry in the world.

In sum, through participation in mission, the church is confirmed in its being the dwelling of the Spirit called to grow in incarnation. Trinitarian faith and life is therefore expressed, shaped and nurtured especially (but certainly not exclusively) in terms of formation and growth in *vocation*.[23] Thus understood and lived out, the church's life of mission orients and motivates the church in the direction of worship and community. In turn, the life of mission is simultaneously undergirded and fostered by the experience and the practices of worship and community.

In summary, according to this revisioning, the church's threefold reason for being consists in: (a) acknowledging and celebrating the reign of God—this is the key to worship; (b) embodying historically and socially the reign of God in its own midst—this is the key to community; and (c) representing, announcing, and participating in the gift, the work, and the promise of God's reign in the world—this is the key to mission. Further, the church ideally maintains a dynamic "ecological balance" among the three arenas and dimensions of ecclesial life and ministry.[24] Figure

---

[23] The analogy and the correlation between mission and vocation is particularly apparent. For the question of how the church helps to awaken and form, prepare for and support people for vocation in today's society, see James W. Fowler, *Becoming Adult, Becoming Christian: Adult Development and Christian Faith* (S. Francisco: Harper & Row, 1984), chapters 4, 5, 6. Also, his discussion of "public church," in *Weaving The New Creation: Stages of Faith and the Public Church* (S. Francisco: Harper Collins, 1991), pp. 155 ff.

[24] We have borrowed the expression "ecological balance" from Howard A. Snyder, who also discusses the main facets of the church's life and work in, *Liberating the Church: The Ecology of Church and Kingdom* (Downers Grove: InterVarsity, 1983), pp. 76-81. Put in simple terms, the normative assumption is that the church must grow simultaneously in the praise and the glory of God as well as in its own edification and in its witness and service in the world. It is understandable, however, that in actual congregations and at opportune times, a given arena often receives special attention in the face of specific challenges and possibilities; in fact, a rhythm of emphases and action often emerges over time as the church seeks to enjoy and to share its vitality wholistically.

1 represents an ecological model of the church in the light of the foregoing discussion.²⁵

Figure 1
The Church and its Threefold Reason for Being

SHAPING THEOLOGICAL EDUCATION

The introduction of this paper indicated that a fundamental assumption at the CTEFC is that *we engage in TE for the sake of the church in the world in the light of God's reign.* The first part of this essay makes the case for the church to be viewed in terms of its trinitarian faith and life²⁶. A number of ramifications follow; we

---

²⁵In this model we attempt to represent the reality of reciprocal relationships among the arenas of ecclesial life and ministry. The arrows in the diagram point in all directions to show the interaction and influence among the three dimensions. The integration in this diagram also illustrates that the three arenas belong together in the same whole (dotted lines are used to indicate that the three cannot be separated neatly from each other) and that they exist together in a dynamic interplay and balance. In other words, the figure points to the ongoing praxis of "ecclesial perichoresis."

²⁶Theologian Catherine Mowry LaCugna says it nicely: "Living trinitarian faith means living God's life: living from and for God, from and for others...living as Jesus Christ lived...according to the power of the Holy

make the case for an ecclesial paradigm in TE, for focus on ministry, and for attention to three interconnected contexts and agendas of TE in terms of overall approach and content. While recognizing that those considerations apply differently to formal, nonformal and congregational settings and modes of TE, we nevertheless claim that they are equally significant in all of them.

An ecclesial paradigm

The first guideline to be affirmed is that, within an Anabaptist framework,[27] TE will be designed in terms of a church-

---

Spirit...Ecclesial life is a way of living in anticipation of the coming reign of God. The church makes a claim...that it is the People of God, Body of Christ, and Temple of the Holy Spirit. The life of the church is to be animated by the life of God: the church is to embody in the world the presence of the risen Christ...the presence, fruits, and work of the Holy Spirit, to be the visible sign of God's reign, of the divine human communion, and the communion of all creatures with one another". In LaCugna, *God for Us: The Trinity and Christian Life* (San Francisco: Harper, 1991), pp. 400-401.

[27]Instead of attempting to define precisely what makes TE "Anabaptist", assuming that that were possible, we prefer to speak of TE within an Anabaptist framework and/or from an Anabaptist perspective. The challenge is here analogous to that of our reflection in other areas such as mission work, justice and peace making, or doing theology itself, also with a supposedly Anabaptist framework and perspective. In fact, our teaching and theological tasks are privileged places where we can consider some of the continuities and commonalities among those and many other kinds of church practices and corresponding reflections. In any event, we do have a number of significant clues in the fashion of core convictions concerning faith and life which are considered normative for the church in all times and places. Thus the church's call to become a truthful sign of God's reign includes a number of dimensions characteristically emphasized in the Anabaptist-Mennonite tradition such as these: the creative as well as forgiving nature of God's grace; the normativeness of Jesus' life and teaching as well as the significance of his death and resurrection for our salvation; the church as a community of covenanted believers symbolized by believers' baptism, congregational discipline, and mutual care; Christian faith viewed and sponsored as the life of discipleship, encompassing all of life; commitment to the way of peace even as a way of confronting evil, and nonparticipation in violence and war; serving others by seeking what makes for genuine peace and by

The Church and Its Theological Education

based model, or ecclesial paradigm. Our biblico-theological foundations point to a vision of TE focused on the church's identity, nature and purpose, namely, its very life and its ministry.[28] A number of key understandings and principles (that is, principles in the sense of dependable guides to the practice of TE) can be thus underscored.

First, we affirm that TE must be viewed, oriented and carried out according to an ecclesial, or church-based, model for several reasons: (a) As indicated in the introduction of this paper, we consider TE a special dimension of the church's larger teaching ministry and at the service of that ministry as well. (b) We consider the church—especially in its concrete, socio-historical embodiment as local congregations, but also in its denominational, global and institutional expressions—to be the main partner, the primary public, and the beneficiary of TE in all its modes and settings. (c) We regard historic faith communities as indispensable contexts of learning and focus of study (that is, substantive curricular content) and scholarly research; we similarly regard church-related institutions, agencies and programs.

Second, the whole TE curriculum—whether in distance TE, congregational biblico-theological education, or formal seminary study—must be approached and developed primarily from the perspective of the reality of the church, its call and reason for being; different dimensions of the curriculum—biblical studies, leadership education, etc.—will consistently keep that concern in

---

inviting people to faith in Jesus Christ; and simplicity in lifestyle. In this view, the relative distinctiveness of the Anabaptist-Mennonite tradition resides in the claim that all of those convictions are essential though not exclusive dimensions of what constitute Christian faithfulness. Therefore, those normative beliefs and practices should occupy a special place in our views and tasks of TE in all its forms, levels and settings.

[28]For a quick view of three alternative approaches to TE specifically related to formal TE in seminaries and divinity schools, see chart in the appendix, taken from the *Ministerial Formation and Theological Education in Mennonite Perspective*. Significant differences can be highlighted between the "ecclesial paradigm" and the "theological" and "ministerial" models (which focus primarily on the nature of theology and on professional ministry respectively as starting points and main foci of concern).

focus. So the overall *curriculum organizing principle*[29] of TE is supplied by the church and its ministry in the world in light of God's reign. A corollary then would be that, in addition to congregations engaging as such in TE, the institutional contexts (such as seminaries, Bible institutes and the like) and programs (such as TEE) will reflect an "ecclesial spirit". They themselves will become faith community settings of teaching and learning that partake, in their own ways, of the church's life and reason for being. More specifically, TE will take place within contexts of authentic evangelical piety and spirituality, genuine Christian ethics and moral behavior, and an epistemology—that is, truth-seeking, discernment and knowing—governed by the very Spirit of God.

Third, TE must be at the service of the faithful church for the purpose of formation and transformation. Its main goal is to support, to strengthen, and to renew the church's life of worship, community, and mission, and to enable and equip the church for the multifaceted tasks of ministry in the world in the light of God's reign. Therefore, a major responsibility for those engaged in TE is to enable the teachers of the church (including, of course, the teachers of teachers, and the church scholars), and to educate pastors, church workers, and other ministering persons. To this focus on ministry we now turn our attention.

Ministry and ministries revisited

Central to the church's reason for being is, indeed, what we have called the multifaceted art and task of ministry.[30] Hence, a

---

[29]"Organizing principle" here means the focal and primary concern of the educational plan and program which determines the actual TE design in any given level or setting. From such a *curriculum organizing principle* a number of specific guidelines follow concerning key questions, such as those related to who are the participants in the TE task and process, what are the goals and objectives to be considered, the approach and methodology which will orient our teaching and learning as well as the content to be dealt with, and so on. A comprehensive and well founded and articulated consideration of those key questions supplies a TE theory (that is, theory in the sense of a systematic set of principles—or "dependable guides"— for the practice of TE).

[30]Within an Anabaptist-Mennonite framework, "ministry" is viewed primarily as the call to all members of the faith community who

second general principle to be affirmed is that, within an Anabaptist framework, TE will contribute to the foundation, education for and evaluation of Christian ministry in terms of enabling for worship, equipping for community, and empowering for mission. The conceptualization that follows has emerged from our own practice of TE and theological reflection in several contexts; it is included here in order to invite further thinking and dialogue on this matter.

In the diagram above (page 21) the manifold Christian ministries of care and discipling, broadly as well as specifically considered,[31] have been placed at the very center because they weave in and out of the church's ongoing life and praxis. As also indicated in the diagram, ministries exist and are carried out in interdependent, reciprocal relationships within the arenas of worship, community, and mission. None of those ministries is an end in itself. Each is seen as serving the church's ultimate purpose of becoming a sacrament of God's love and reign. And all the various ministries contribute to foster and sustain the manifold experiences and practices constitutive of the church's trinitarian life and faith in any given socio-historical and cultural context. It should be clear that no narrow, one-to-one correspondence between

---

are endowed with manifold gifts to participate in divers forms of Christian ministry. And ministry is also understood as the task of those persons called and appointed to ministerial offices such as pastors, teachers, evangelists, mission workers, administrators and others. These ministerial offices assume a special calling from God and church, certain discernible gifts bestowed, and a continuing role and accountability together with the cultivation of skills required for effective service. Obviously, TE must be concerned with both views and practices regarding ministry.

[31] On the one hand, the expression "care and discipling" denotes the widest possible reference to the *content* of Christian ministry regardless of form, mode and setting, and regardless of the ecclesiastical status and the credentials of the ministering persons. On the other hand, that expression serves as an umbrella for a variety of recognizable tasks such as pastoral care and counseling, teaching, mentoring, spiritual direction, music ministry, administration, and so on. Obviously, ministries also extend beyond congregational life in a narrow sense, including (together with those already mentioned, which also can and should have an "outreach" dimension and a "centrifugal" direction) such tasks as prophetic and evangelistic witness, serving the poor, working for justice and peace, caring for the earth and the environment, etc.

specific ministries and the various ecclesial practices is being assumed or proposed. Every form of ministry is responsible for doing its part to establish and sustain the whole complex of ecclesial practices; likewise, every form of ministry is itself some constellation of all of the practices. Thus, every one of those practices should contribute to every form of ministry, and every form of ministry must be related to the whole variety of practices.[32]

According to those considerations, in the call and the reality of the church ministries serve a threefold purpose: *ministries take place in order to enable persons for worship, to equip them for community, and to empower them for mission.* Conversely, each arena or dimension of the church encourages and sets directions for ministry in all its forms, modes and settings. A key task of practical and pastoral theology is, therefore, to help identify specific ways in which such a threefold purpose may be focused and carried out, whether in the settings of counseling, teaching, or in any other type of ministry. For example, ministry objectives and tasks can be clustered as follows. (a) *Enabling for worship*: to become more aware of and open to God's presence and grace; to appropriate the biblical story and biblical faith; to gain understanding of the history and significance of Christian worship; to appreciate the role of ritual, symbol, story, music and other arts in worship; to learn the practices and disciplines of prayer, confession/repentance, offering/giving, and others; to acquire skills for worship participation and leading, etc. (b) *equipping for community*: to help persons become aware of self/selves in God's presence; to embrace the biblical story of God's people and the historical tradition of the church; to gain interpersonal skills such as listening and communicating effectively; to learn to mediate conflicts and to

---

[32]As rightly stated in the *Growing in the Life of the Christian Faith* document: "Practically speaking, the adequacy of a form of ministry can be evaluated in part by the degree to which all of those practices are involved in and sustained by that form of ministry. When some are missing, an evaluation of the way in which that ministry is carried out may very well be called for. For as each of the practices is increasingly built into every form of ministry and as the quality of the community's active participation in the practices is enhanced and enriched in and by that form of ministry, the one ministry of the whole church is itself made stronger." (pp. 31-32)

resolve disputes; to develop attitudes and aptitudes for all forms of family life such as parenting or singleness; to learn and to grow in mutual support and aid, mutual discipling, group and community leadership; to genuinely embrace marginalized groups and persons (the unschooled, disabled, mentally ill, victims of abuse, and others), etc.; (c) *empowering for mission*: to learn to recognize the Spirit's voice and work in the world; to receive and share God's loving invitation to good news/good reality in Jesus Christ; to develop awareness, sensitivity, compassion and solidarity in the face of prejudice due to gender, sexuality, race, culture, etc.; to join the struggle against structural injustice and oppression; to share and give generously, to serve the poor, weak, disabled, and marginalized, to relate responsibly to the non-human environment, etc.

In light of our TE concerns we have just redefined ministry functionally as the multifaceted art and task of enabling for worship, equipping for community, and empowering for mission. Such ministry in turn needs to be correlated with the main contexts and agendas for theological reflection and education as well as briefly discussed in the next section.

Three contexts and four agendas for theological education

Our fundamental common assumption is that *we engage in TE for the sake of the church in the world in the light of God's reign.* Implicit in that statement are three main, interrelated contexts and agendas of TE: the ecclesial context and the agenda of the church, including historical considerations; the socio-cultural context and agenda of our world, broadly as well as narrowly speaking; and the context of God's commonwealth of freedom, justice and peace and God's agenda revealed in Word and Spirit. Due consideration to each of these interrelated contexts/agendas is essential if TE is to be both faithful to the gospel as well as pertinent to our faith communities' situations in history. This third general principle encompasses the necessity of a manifold faith and educational commitment on our part, as reflected in the three sets of interconnected contexts or loci for theological reflection and TE represented in figure 2 below.

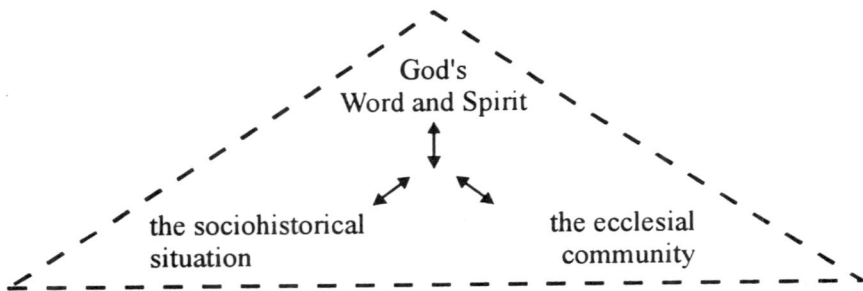

Figure 2
Three Contexts of Theological Education

Theological reflection helps us to clarify major concerns of the church's teaching ministry, including TE, regarding the interpretation of the Scriptures and the work of God's Spirit, the nature and purpose of the church, and the Christian view of the culture and the historical situation. Given our biblico-theological foundations, the three vectors in the diagram must converge in the gospel of the reign of God (which points to the gift, the promise, and the expectations and demands of the inbreaking reality of the new creation in the light of Jesus Christ). Thus the reign of God is not imagined merely as a transcendent, as well as other-worldly, eschatological reality, and it is not located somehow only in God's mind and heart; no, it is affirmed as God's present will and dream, the gift and promise of the new creation in Christ. The Bible does not merely present a clear definition or complete picture of God's commonwealth of *shalom*; rather the Holy Scriptures provide indispensable "windows"—clues and illustrations of divine and human creative, liberating, and renewing work—through the narratives, symbols, teachings, and confessions that point to the life of freedom, justice and peace. For its part the church is not merely identified with the reign of God, yet it is called to concretely become a foretaste, a beachhead or sacrament of divine life emerging in real life. Finally, no social order can ever be equated with God's reign, yet God's will is to be realized and discerned in the midst of historical, sociocultural and politico-economic structures[33].

The interrelations of those vectors and the three contexts emerge in what we call the *agendas* that must inform our educational endeavors (both for "discipleship" and for "apostleship") at all levels and in all forms of the church's teaching ministry. The diagram in figure 3, which builds on the previous one, can help us appreciate the dynamics involved.

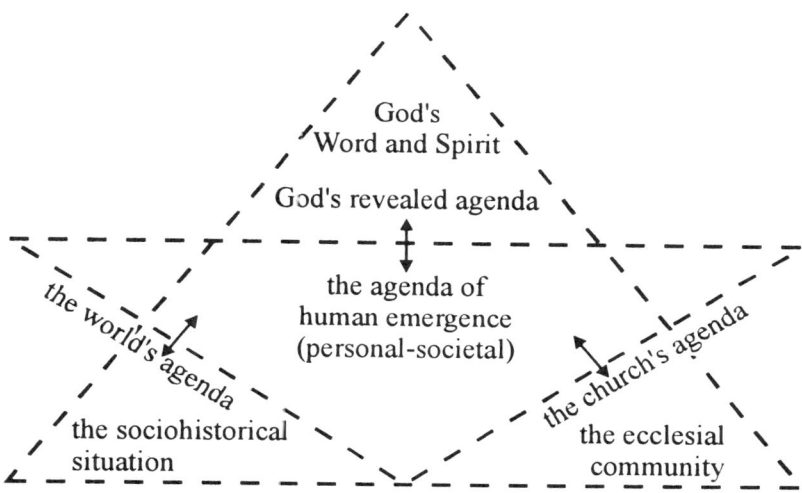

Figure 3
Four Agendas in Theological Education

The Spirit-led discernment of God's creative, liberating and renewing work for the sake of *shalom* in the light of the Bible and

---

[33]In the case of the North American context, for example, recent attention to the socio-historical situation can be documented in a number of unpublished papers prepared for consideration in regard to TE, such as the following: "Shaping the Mennonite Church Vision in Post-Modern Reality" (Edward Stoltzfus and others, 1989); "God and the People of God in a Postmodern World" (Howard J. Loewen and others, 1989); "The Church and Education in the Post-Modern Age" (John E. Toews, 1994); "The Implications of North American Culture for Pastoral Leadership in the 21st Century" (Gerald Shenk, 1996).

the living Christ corresponds to what is called "God's revealed agenda" of Word and Spirit, in dialogue with the other two. The tradition and the living story of God's people, including the life and ministry of the ecclesial community today (from local congregations to the global church) constitute the core of the "agenda of the church", to be considered also in connection with the other two. And the natural and social context with its cultural, political and economic dimensions, comprise the "world's agenda", also in association with the other two. Obviously, all of these dimensions are interrelated in diverse ways and also are in certain tension with each other. We have added a fourth dimension—the "agenda of human emergence"—deliberately placed at the center, which signifies the life, learning, growth, and transformation of persons and faith communities who participate in the educational ministry or who are affected in some way by it.

A key to process and content in TE: "hermeneutical circulation"

The fourth and final general principle we wish to affirm relates to contexts and agendas, with questions pertaining to process (How shall we do TE?), and content (What shall be learned and taught in TE?). It can be stated simply thus: the process of hermeneutical circulation is the principal axis of our task. This provides the clue for the structural content—that is, approach and methodology—as integrating factor; it is also the key to substantive content—that is, the thematic agenda—of the TE curriculum. Given the leading presence of the Holy Spirit as Divine Teacher and Christians' personal commitment to faithful following of Jesus Christ—that is, obedience as epistemological principle—a multidimensional conversation will result among the three factors in hermeneutical circulation: the text of the Bible, the context of the hemeneutic faith community, and the "pre-text" of the world in which we live. The process thus underscored is communal, dialogical, collaborative, and discipleship/ministry-oriented (figure 4)[34].

---

[34]For this way of conceptualizing the process of hermeneutical circulation we are indebted to Latin American sources, especially to the work of Carlos Mesters in Brazil. See his article, "The Use of the Bible in

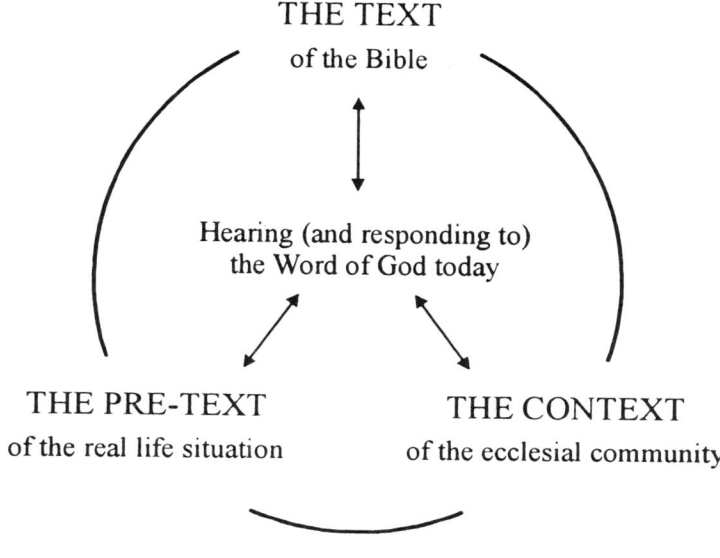

Figure 4
Hermeneutical Circulation as Multiway Conversation

Each of those three dimensions—text, context, and pre-text—is indispensable for authentically being in dialogue with God's Word today. In other terms, the gospel message must be creatively discerned, appropriated and communicated amidst a conversation that engages the biblical text in its own context together with a critical reading of the surrounding historical and cultural reality and with the ecclesial community itself (including both local and global history/tradition) assumed to be committed to the ethics and the politics of God. In the last analysis, the purpose of such a process of hermeneutical circulation is not so much to arrive at a flawless biblical interpretation, but rather to enable each other to grow in the interpretation and transformation of life in the light of Jesus Christ. Consequently, the Bible is viewed as the normative standard for faithfulness of life, ministry and thought.

---

the Christian Communities of the Common People", in Sergio Torres and John Eagleson, eds. *The Challenge of Basic Christian Communities* (Maryknoll: Orbis, 1981).

We affirm in this way the centrality of Scripture as the text of the church, as God's Word written for all peoples. A consistent hermeneutical practice is essential to reconcile, to integrate and to mutually enhance "Christian education" for discipleship, broadly speaking, and TE as education for apostleship. Such a hermeneutical process fills a key role in regard to the church's threefold reason for being—worship, community, and mission. Bible study and interpretation will normally happen in the framework of a prayerful and worshipful spirit. Reading and dialogue around Scripture then become not only a process of observation, analysis and application, but also a means of celebration and adoration, an experience conducive to worship for God's covenant people. Simultaneously, Christian disciples gathered around the Bible in any given setting will nurture their faith and grow in the life of communion with one another as the body of Christ; and they, as the temple of the Holy Spirit, will also become empowered for witness and service, for their vocation and mission.

CONCLUSION

In this essay we explored the place and the function of TE in terms of the first goal of the Barrackpore Consultation, which was to promote reflection on the broad vision of how TE contributes to strengthen and renew Anabaptist churches for their life of worship, community, and mission. We accomplished the task by focusing on the meaning and the main ramifications of our response to the question, "Why do we engage in TE?"—*We engage in TE for the sake of the church in the world in the light of the reign of God*. Given our biblical-theological grounding, we started with a discussion on the church's identity, character, and reason for being. We thus suggested that our view of the church must include consideration of the trinitarian base and structure of our Christian faith. We proposed a number of principles to serve as dependable guides to our practice and reflection upon TE in all forms, modes and levels. It is our hope and our prayer that we may together further the reflection and discussion, and that our overall

PROYECTO RENUEVO

El Seminario Anabautista Latinoamericano, SEMILLA

otorga el presente

Diploma de reconocimiento

a

Angie Yoder

por su participación dinámica en el Primer Encuentro de Instituciones Teológicas, "Educación teológica desde la visión anabautista, abriendo caminos de unidad e intercambio en los desafíos contemporáneos" realizado en la Ciudad de Guatemala, del 26-28 de noviembre de 2007.

Willi Hugo Pérez Lemus
Rector.

Linda Shelly
Directora para América Latina.

Sandra Campos
Presidenta Junta Directiva.

collaboration may enrich TE in the days and years ahead. May God bless our work.

Appendix

	Theological Paradigm
	From an analysis of the nature of theology to the nature and reform of theological education. *The seminary is a **graduate school**.*
Perspective	The TE* curriculum is approached from the nature of theology. TE is seen primarily as an education in theological inquiry.
Focus	Doing theology involves development of virtue and character. TE is linked with personal and vocational formation; concern with critical inquiry, vision and discernment; formation of pastoral theologians.
Main purpose	To develop the habit of theological inquiry, i.e., development of critical judgment in several dimensions (e.g. discernment of the nature, truth, appropriateness of Christian witness).
Strengths	Because it views theology (and the habit of theological inquiry) as closely related to faith itself, the "theological paradigm" connects "Christian education" and "theological education"; indeed, theological education continues and deepens Christian education. It concentrates on the normative questions facing the church (essentially related to its identity, life and purpose, in the light of the reign of God) regarding background and perspective for discernment and assessment of the tasks of ministry. Theological education's primary concern is to normatively clarify what it means to be a faithful church in the midst of history.
Weaknesses	Risks becoming an "academic" paradigm (pejoratively speaking): Focus on development of the habit of discernment may result in failure to grasp the concrete dimensions of TE. Whereas theological inquiry is central to the exercise of ministry, there are elements of ministerial praxis not covered by the requisite discernments of critical inquiry. The "habit of ministerial practice" cannot be reduced to the "habit of critical inquiry." The practice of ministry, in other words, is not identical to the practice of good theology (in the sense of an almost exclusive focus on both discernment and critical inquiry as well as the intelligibility and credibility of the content of faith).

*TE: Theological education

Ecclesial Paradigm	*Ministerial Paradigm*
From the church's identity, life and purpose for being to the nature and reform of theological education. *The seminary is both a **graduate** and a **professional school.***	From a theological/professional view of ministry and its distinctive nature to the nature and reform of theological education. *The seminary is a **professional school.***
The TE* curriculum is approached from the perspective of the nature and the purpose of the church.	The TE* curriculum is approached from the nature of Christian ministry (sacramental and/or professional view of ministry).
TE is linked primarily with the formation and transformation of the faithful church in the world in the light of God's reign.	TE is linked primarily with formation and training of Christian ministers, according to a sacramental or professional view.
To support and renew the church's life of worship, community, and mission.	To prepare, equip and enable the servants/leaders and other church workers for the tasks of carrying out their ministerial vocations in and/or on behalf of the church.
The ecclesial paradigm attempts to create and maintain a creative tension and balance between the theological and the ministerial paradigms. Hence, there is deliberate and carefully fashioned work to blend, synthesize and integrate the contributions and strengths of both the "theological" and the "ministerial" approaches to theological education. The church is to be empowered by the faithful, competent leadership of servant/ministers for participating in God's work in the world . Thus, TE fosters the formation and training of church workers whose reflective practice of ministry assumes a normative framework and perspective within and from which the church's life and task are to be viewed and carried out.	Because of its focus on ministry, this paradigm keeps central the actual situations, challenges and possibilities of the work of ministry. It underscores the empowering function of TE for Christian ministry by concentrating on growth in specific knowledge and skills, abilities and competencies as well as personal qualifications and benchmarks. It contributes to curriculum development by underscoring the foundational and partner-like roles of "context," non-theological disciplines and fields as they intersect with the practice of ministry and with theological reflection on ministry. It seeks to overcome the theory and practice dualism by promoting theological education for the formation and training of "reflective practitioners."
Risks becoming a "religious community" paradigm (pejoratively speaking) : The ingrownness of the church may be fostered, betraying an ecclesiocentric focus (too much concern with the church's own needs rather than being properly attentive to the needs of the world that the church is supposed to know, love and serve in Christ's name). An ecclesial focus risks too much emphasis on denominational identity and preservation and, more specifically, denominational policies and parochial expectations, thus losing its creative and prophetic potential.	Risks becoming a "clerical" paradigm (pejoratively speaking): The concrete parochial expectations of ministers and the wishes of church leadership may become normative rather than those criteria demanded by good theology and the purpose of the church. That is, empowering of the clergy rather than of faith communities becomes the focus. There is further tendency to rely uncritically upon the functionalist and developmentalist assumptions inherent in the clerical paradigm which promote an individualistic view of ministry as well as the fragmentation of the TE curriculum.

The Task and the Challenges of Theological Education

*Our **central task** is to reveal Christ, "until all of us come ...to the measure of the full stature..." (Eph. 4:13)*
Our desire is that through teaching,
the character of Christ might be reflected
in persons and communities.

*Our **theme** is from 2 Tim. 2:2, "...entrust to faithful people who will be able to teach others as well." The **educational goal** is to equip the saints*
for the work of ministry,
for building up the body (Eph. 4:12).
Every believer has a part in Christ's ministry.

*The **purpose** of our theological education must be:*
...both to support the ministries and to extend the body;
...to enable our faith communities to think theologically about their contexts from the standpoint of faith.

The church must pray that God will send workers for the harvest. The church must also pray that the workers can meet the challenges which will face them in the field of harvest. God has given the vision to us; now we must respond by providing the necessary resources and skills for the harvest.

*Only when we are willing to live in **the tension between vision and current reality**, and experience the mutual correction that comes from that tension,*
will we be able as a church
to see and walk in transforming ways
in the light of God's reign.

2

Congregational Theological Education: Congregational Education

Leonor de Méndez (Guatemala)

The formation of persons at a congregational level has the objective of conforming individuals and communities to the image of Jesus. Formal and informal leadership training, then, is a tool which theological institutions offer to the faith communities. These institutions have reason to exist if one of their final objectives is that congregations be enriched through their teaching, and that the educational ministry produce life and health in the congregations.

I recognize that each region and culture differs in their assignment of educating the church, but there are similar necessities and problems that are common to us and for which we can unite our efforts.

I want to describe briefly our educational situation in Central America by focusing on the three following aspects: the obstacles, successes, and our hopes for the future.

CENTRAL AMERICAN REALITY

Obstacles

Lack of materials. It is always difficult to find good teaching material. There are many materials in Spanish from other theological currents, but they generally do not help to strengthen our Anabaptist thought. They frequently propose an "easy" gospel which lacks depth, which spiritualizes, and which is indifferent to our Central American reality.

The themes of much of this material do not relate to our everyday life with faith, nor do they connect reality with spirituality. This fact leads us to reduce learning simply to a spiritual plane which does not permit teaching to be grounded in reality and daily life, nor bring forth concrete changes.

There are attractive materials for children and youth with beautiful pictures in full color, activities and games, but they also present a gospel very different from the reality of our marginal barrios, indigenous populations which do not have rights to the land, or street children who go to sleep hungry every night.

The lack of good educational materials becomes even more apparent when we look for material for specific groups such as single persons, young married couples, women, the elderly, or on such topics as divorce, second marriages, or AIDS.

In addition, there is a big cost connected to the majority of existing materials and many of the small churches do not have sufficient funds to buy them. The academic level of many materials is also high and complicated, and many of our teachers do not have adequate preparation to be able to use them.

Lack of teacher preparation. For the most part our teachers have little biblical knowledge. They repeat theological concepts they have learned and read without having adequate criteria stemming from their own experience with the Bible. Many times they have neither the resources nor the time to prepare themselves well. They improvise topics and do not follow an educational sequence. They lack a reflection which contextualizes the Scriptures so that they can provide answers and parameters for those who hear.

Inadequate methods. Teaching becomes repetitive and unchallenging because we often teach everyone at the same level, without adequate development, progression, or attempts to relate content to real life. This pattern is due in part to the fact that many brothers and sisters do not read. Teachers use a magisterial teaching style in which the teacher knows everything, and the congregation only receives what is given to them without being able to become involved in dialogue and reflection. There is little creativity and knowledge on the part of the teachers to incorporate new participatory methodologies.

Inadequate connection between theory and practice. Those brothers and sisters who have been in the church a long time know the biblical teaching and theory, but they do not know how to *put into practice* what they have learned. There is a tendency to separate spiritual life from real life, and not see both as integrally related. The churches are often not profoundly involved in the life of the people. They do not naturally initiate small projects according to the real needs of the communities, where members could put into practice what they have been learning. They do not give space for new leaders, therefore persons do not see a reason why they should prepare to serve and teach.

There is little motivation in the congregation for teaching. When other activities are offered in the churches, people respond, but there is often an absence when programming Christian education, Bible studies, and other teaching moments. We seem to lack goals of "why" or "for what reason" we should study or develop ourselves. People learn only for learning's sake, and in this routine a vitality for the gospel is lost.

Worship and music. Normally we use an hour once a week for congregational education. This is a short time in order to accomplish any serious formation of the people. We recognize that formation does not occur only in the formal educational moment. There are a variety of experiences that form a part of learning, such as song content, how we celebrate the Lord's Supper, times of sharing and intercession, our rejection of the use of symbols. In not giving importance, balance or an adequate focus to these spaces, we deprive ourselves of the opportunity for integrated learning through other experiences.

Successes

Alongside this panorama which looks quite negative we also have hope. Many churches are exploring alternatives that take them closer to a Central American Anabaptist way such as the three indicated below.

Teaching content that responds to our actual reality. At the present time we are attempting to have our teaching mesh with our social, political, and economic reality. We want to contextualize the Bible within our Central American reality by means of our own re-reading of the Bible with a focus on commitment and obedience.

Anabaptist identity. We have been acquiring an Anabaptist identity, but the process has been slow. In this search, we have paid a price. Many have not accepted this posture, and have left. This new identity has also affected our form of leadership. We see leadership and authority as a shared assignment that avoids hierarchies and does not permit power to be centered in one person. It is inclusive, not exclusive.

We have seen the need to revise the content of the songs we sing and what we do in our worship, so that they express more adequately our culture and way of being. We are further reflecting on the cost of faithful discipleship and serious commitment to an ethic for life. To be church calls us to much more than simply being a group of persons. We commit ourselves to mutual submission, correction, support and blessing as a body of Christ. We are very conscious that our reason for existing is not only for our own internal advantage, but to extend the Kingdom of God into the community.

Search for a participatory methodology. We have achieved in part some alternative teaching methodologies that have motivated people to share of their own wealth of experience, and helped them discover and share their own potential. We have adjusted the level of formal theological education to more popular levels so that more brothers and sisters can study, and we have prepared materials accordingly. SEMILLA—The Central American Anabaptist Seminary and Theological education program—was born because of the need for Anabaptist education at a congregational level. It currently includes a department that promotes formation and preparation of adequate materials for the congregations.

Hopes for the future

The task and the challenges of congregational theological education in our context point to a number of priorities for us to consider. Four of those practical priorities are briefly discussed in the next paragraphs.

To promote biblical knowledge. We want to help people comprehend the Bible through inductive study and other participatory methods so that the congregation, as it reflects on the Word, can appropriate it, and at any given moment the Scripture becomes normal life practice. We do not want to impart biblical knowledge merely as an intellectual exercise, but rather to help believers to know the Scriptures so that their reflection fills the vacuum and responds to personal and community needs. Our intention is not to simply transmit stories or fundamental truths, but to guide and facilitate a process in which the community discovers the truth for itself, applies it and makes it a part of its own life.

For example, the rich youth (Matt 7:27) knew and obeyed the commandments, which is more than many do today. But at Christ's request that he *do* them, he could not respond. Matthew tells us that the youth fell and his ruin was great. He knew, but he could not do. Our teaching has to illuminate our ethic, practice, discipleship, and mission.

A content that promotes life. We want to develop a curriculum that is based on the central principles that teach us how

Congregational Theological Education

to live the Kingdom of God now. We need a vision for a curricular plan that takes us toward short and long-term integrated growth.

Integrated teacher preparation. We would like teachers to be better prepared with basic courses such as hermeneutics, church history, introduction to Old and New Testaments, and methodology. These studies would help in their own comprehension of the biblical content, and their way of transmitting them to the congregations.

Accessible education. Education should be simple and attractive in its content and presentation, but with cycles of development so that it will not be repetitive.

CONCLUSION

Our desire is that through the teaching, the character of Christ might be reproduced in each member in his or her daily living, that a positive attitude of commitment and following Christ might be born in each one, and that each one might know the cost and seriousness of discipleship.

We desire for the church to be built, nurtured, strengthened, and guided through its comprehension and application of the Scriptures in daily life, and not only through a merely intellectual knowledge of them. In order to reach these goals, we are aware that we must:

* Motivate learning
* Invest time and effort in the preparation of excellent congregational leaders
* Re-read the Scriptures within our own context and reality
* Provide materials for popular levels, with methodologies that encourage and enable persons to search, reflect, and obey what they learn and know
* Study content and topics that relate to our everyday life so that they guide us to concrete, pertinent, and faithful actions
* Know the ethical values of the reign of God so that as Anabaptists, our theological richness becomes known and is lived out

Our central task is to reveal Christ. As Paul said to the Colossians, "Teaching everyone in all wisdom, so that we may present everyone mature in Christ" (Col 1:28) and to the Ephesians, "Until all of us come...to the measure of the full stature of Christ (Eph 4:13).

RESPONSE

Cathy Motuli Mputu (Congo)

Introduction

In relationship with the presentation about education in local congregations of Anabaptist churches in Central America, we note that this work is very important and the contents of the work connects with the situation of our churches in Africa. In fact, both formal and more particularly informal training must be seen as indispensable to strengthen our members. Almost all the major points in Leonor's paper can be found in our churches as well. An example is the much-too-limited participation of women in training activities.

What we have in common

Lack of materials. It is true that we have little appropriate material, yet we find ways to work. For certain categories of instructions, no materials exist. We do have a department of Christian literature which would be able to prepare material adapted to our context, but financial difficulties and lack of equipment make this department ineffective.

Lack of training of teachers. Most of our teachers take on responsibilities because of their experience and seniority in the church rather than because of their pedagogical competence. As a consequence, pedagogical knowledge is poorly transmitted to other teachers. The church is encouraging congregational members to be trained in theological and biblical institutions.

Inadequate methods. In our churches, often the teacher teaches and everyone else sits as a passive recipient. Teachers are only used to this "ex cathedra" (expository) method. Creativity is seldom used in their teaching. The motivation of teachers is further inhibited because the materials they have available are not well adapted and old.

Insufficient links between theory and practice. Our churches include many members who are not strong in faith nor greatly involved. This means that many of them are not growing spiritually. They attend church as a formality. Despite the length of time that they have been part of the church, the lives of some of our members do not reflect the gospel.

Congregational Theological Education

Lack of enthusiasm for teaching. We note this problem most of all during Bible studies, debates, and sessions of intercessory prayer. Our members prefer activities such as choir rehearsals to Bible studies, claiming that the latter require too much intellectual ability. It goes without saying that the level of formal educational background varies widely within the church.

Praise and music. Our members like this aspect of our gatherings. For them, praising means lively singing, dancing and jumping; when it is time to move to other parts of worship, everyone becomes discouraged. It is as if we come to church only to sing. So during worship we give no more than 20 or 30 minute to preaching and teaching. There are often four or five choirs in each congregation. Unfortunately, these choirs are not trained and mostly imitate the messages and styles of other denominations. It is difficult to speak of Christian choir members in our congregations, since many of these members do not offer a positive witness. Those of us who are teachers and leaders in the congregation often do not pay enough attention to the songs sung by our choirs, since we never participate in their practices. Thus some of the songs edify neither the members of the choir themselves nor the rest of the congregation because they lack biblical content.

What is particular to our churches

Women in training. Participation of women in training in our churches is quite limited. This situation is caused by several factors: a) many women have very little formal education; b) many women suffer from inferiority complexes because of some of our customs and traditions; c) some women are not interested.

Scattered energies. Often the lack of overall planning on the part of those responsible for the work of the congregation means that what little training which is offered is not well coordinated and oriented from a common perspective. Therefore a great deal of effort and energy is wasted.

Proposals

Given the realities as described in Central American churches as well as those briefly discussed above in regard to our own churches, I would like to make the following suggestions:

* That teacher-trainers be well instructed in Anabaptist theology and that they use such reflection as much as

possible in relationship with the reality of their own contexts.

* That pedagogical strategies (for example, participatory methods, types of teaching materials) be developed so that theoretical knowledge corresponds with the realities of the daily life of congregational members, and that congregational members be motivated to participate in greater numbers in teacher-training activities.

* That specific groups of members (for example, women, single people, children) be considered in teaching situations which respond to their particular situations. Women, for example, need training which takes into account their domestic and spiritual situations, so that they can grow in participation in the church, their contexts, and in the broader society.

* That congregations take the responsibility to begin programs of literacy training in their midst so that members can improve their ability to read and understand the Word of God.

RESPONSE

Mikha Joedhiswara (Indonesia)

The Context: Challenge to Theological Education in the Congregation

The common denominator between Asia and the rest of the Third World is its suffering in the face of overwhelming poverty. The specific character defining countries in Asia among other poor countries is its multifaceted religiosity. These two prominent features must be taken seriously into account in congregational theological education.

The socio-economic situation throughout Asia is characterized by widespread poverty and deprivation. Hence, it is sad to see that many of the Christians who go regularly to church, attending prayer services or Sunday worship, hardly ever reflect seriously on the immense human misery. It is puzzling that so many who attend Church are so little concerned about people who are politically oppressed, socially alienated, economically exploited and kept uneducated in cultural and intellectual matters. The churches have tended to understand the church's mission in very individualistic terms. The church has been slow in becoming aware of its responsibility to participate with God in the mission of social, economic and political renewal. Because a great deal of theological thinking is individualistic in orientation, the social aspects of the Kingdom of God, of sin, conversion, and salvation, have been neglected. Social aspects are often considered "merely" human, humanitarian, horizontal, and "merely" natural, not related to the spiritual, to God.

"A theology bereft of social analysis" and "an excessively theoretical theology" largely influence our churches. Faith is commonly understood as knowledge and faithfulness to inherited doctrines, that is, from the past and from the West. Modern biblical studies have concentrated increasingly on the past, interpreting biblical documents to determine their original meaning and relating the formulations of faith in the ancient world to their original context. Far less attention is given to how to understand and proclaim the gospel to the world today, to analyzing the opportunities and problems for Christian faith in the modern world, and indeed to asking what God is doing in our times. The practicable result of this is that faith becomes alienated from and irrelevant to its context; *orthodoxy* is emphasized and separated from *orthopraxis*.

Asian religiosity, expressed in Buddhism, Hinduism, Confucianism, Taoism, Shintoism, Islam, and many other religions that have arisen on Asian soil, still holds sway over the people. Religious thought patterns and social organizations based on religion are so much a part of Asian societies. It is impossible to speak meaningfully to the Asian context without taking its religious ethos into account. Christianity can no longer ignore the presence and influence of other faiths or the culture and spirituality they have created in Asian societies.

Christians in Asian countries, except Philippines and Korea, are a small minority. As part of the human community, the life and destiny of the Christian community in Asia is bound up with the socio-economic situation of the total community. As a minority, Christians must participate with others in building their nations and in seeking solutions to pressing social and economic problems. As individuals, Christians share their lives with neighbors of other faiths at school, play, and work.

The relation between Islam and Christianity (in Indonesia) needs to receive attention on a more empirical level. Seen from the viewpoint of the competition in seeking and defending their followers, the relation between Islam and Christianity contain many problems and potential conflicts These two religions were characterized by misunderstanding, mistrust and even hatred to one another. The attitude of superiority in each of these religions is very great. Therefore, the relation between them always tends to be polemical, apologetical, and antithetical. This condition can continue to develop into an explosive situation. If the church is going to continue their religious teachings which are set forth in an absolute way, to oppose the teaching and beliefs of others, it should be known that the problems and dangers it will raise will be greater than the benefits. Non-Christians are automatically angry, upset and insulted if they read or hear that their religion is considered to be false, full of demonic or satanic aspects, full of deep intuition of sin and guilt, and lacking the intuition of God, holiness, and righteousness. As a result of that anger, various physical conflicts have emerged.

A major challenge to Christians in Asia is overcoming the image of being instruments and agents of Western colonialism and imperialism, as they are perceived by other faiths. This perception is not mistaken, since Christianity came to Asia together with the forces of Western colonialism and imperialism. Christians need to make a serious attempt to answer this accusation by showing deep concern for an involvement in finding solutions to Asian suffering. "Christ in the colonial era" was taught, not as a friend to all, especially the poor and the oppressed, but as the emperor, the judge, and the universal government that controlled everything. Mission and imperialism were intertwined, ensuring that the gospel of Christ would be misinterpreted.

It seems that the Church has not been able to penetrate into the minds and hearts of most Asian people. The idea that becoming a Christian means accepting a new life, a life that must forsake "the life of the past remains." The life of the past in this context means a life that is bound by culture and cultural traditions. Thus, a Christian must no longer be bound or even "attracted" and "practice" so many things that are considered "non-Christian" and must accept only the new life in Christ. This life in Christ, as we now realize, is not culture-free, but culture-laden. It is in fact, wrapped up in the Western (Dutch) cultural forms and traditions: clothes (dress), music, liturgy, even thoughts (theology, dogma, or the church doctrines), which are all alien to the people's minds and hearts and the practices of daily life.

A Relevant Theological Education in the Congregation

The paper presented by Leonor de Méndez underlined a premise that to be significant to the contemporary Third World, congregational education must seek to take seriously the encounter between people's life and the Word of God. It is my belief that the gospel is universal and at the same time is also particular. The universal nature of the gospel should make it possible and desirable for all peoples, to accept its message. At the same time, the particularity of the gospel should make it possible and desirable that it be understood in every particular culture, with that culture's own cultural forms and traditions. If the gospel is universal it should be possible to be deeply rooted and to grow in every culture.

Contextualization of congregational education, with an emphasis on ministerial formation in context, has been a major emphasis in the presentation. It is a strongly Christian voice, speaking out of its journey with God and reinterpreting the Christian tradition considering its context. It is a way of understanding the Christian faith, not only on the basis of Scripture and tradition, but also on the basis of concrete culturally conditioned human experience. Christian communities should analyze with objectivity the situation which is proper to their country to shed on it the light of the gospel's unalterable words and to draw principles or reflections, norms or judgement, and directives of action from the teaching of the church. It seeks not only to reinterpret Western thought from an Asian perspective ("adaptation theology") or merely to respond to the gospel with traditional or native culture ("indigenization theology"). Contextualization, while not ignoring this, takes into account the processes of secularization, technology, and the struggle for human justice, which characterize the historical moment of the nations in the Third World. Contextualization carefully distinguishes between false forms of contextualizing and authentic contextualization. False contextualization yields to uncritical accommodation, to a form of culture-faith. Authentic contextualization is always prophetic, arising from a genuine encounter between God's Word and God's world, and moving toward the purpose of challenging the situation through rootedness in and commitment to a given historical moment. Therefore we need a participatory methodology in congregational education by doing contextual theology in a hermeneutic spiral with close relationship between elements of the following points:

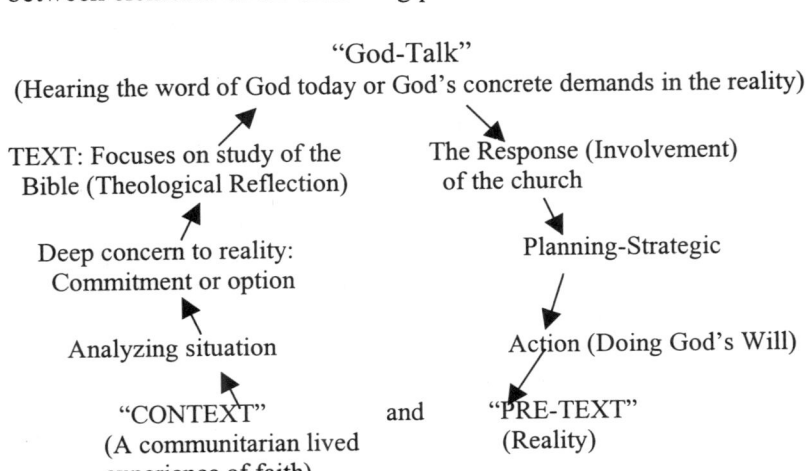

Theological Education in the Congregation in a Multifaith Context

The purpose of theological education in the congregation is to enable the congregation to think theologically about the context from the standpoint of faith. What does the congregational education process need in the context of religious pluralism, so that our congregations are empowered to live and witness within their community effectively?

Our congregational education activities need to include the following goals: (1) To create a better understanding of our own faith in relation to other faiths; (2) to develop greater respect for the faith of our neighbors; (3) to overcome the fear of losing our own faith in our encounter with other faiths; (4) to create trust with people of other faiths; (5) to deal with situations of tension that arise when one faith confronts another; (6) to arrive at a more human understanding of the world as a whole. The activities of Christian education in this context need to include the following kingdom values: (1) Respect for human dignity; (2) honor of human rights; (3) clear understanding of justice, peace, and the integrity of creation; (4) God's loving care for us all.

TABLE 1: Sunday School and Day school

Target Groups by Age	Method	Resources	Facilitators
4-5,6-8	Story telling, games, plays, visiting gardens, festivals of other religions, songs and cartoons	Bible, story books, organized games and playgrounds, cartoon films and books, coloring books, icons.	Sunday school teachers who are given special training, parents, pastors
9-11	Research & group work on the practices of other religions, group activities, exposure programs to other faiths, formal education in the classroom about other faiths	Textbooks, coloring books, booklets and pamphlets about the faiths and practices of other people.	Day-school and Sunday school teachers
12-14	Awareness building about the values in other religions, study of basic teaching of other religions, exposure programs (visits to temples, mosques, etc.)	Booklets about other religions, stories of the heroes of all religions	Day school, Sunday School and School teachers.
15-17	Conferences, study circles, camps, exposure programmes.	Camp manuals, conference materials, books about the faith and practices of other religions.	Sunday & day school teachers, friends from other religions.

TABLE II: Parish-Related Groups

Target Groups	Method	Resources	Facilitators
Bible Study Groups	Study of the Bible and comparative study with other sacred books	Bibles of several versions, commentaries, concordance, sacred books of other religions	Experts in the area of Christian faith and the faith of other religions.
Youth Group	Conferences, camps projects and exposure programs with other faiths	Bible, conference materials which include booklets about other religions, common community projects	Leaders and counselors
Women's Group	community activities, visits to homes, literacy programme for women, prayer meetings, visits to the sick in hospitals	Local materials, embroidery and cooking, street cleaning, literacy books. Hospital visiting groups.	Women leaders, from local parish and from other religions.

TABLE III: Formal Organizations

Target Groups	Method	Resources	Facilitators
Theological Colleges	Regular courses about other religions, study of the sacred books of other religions, extension programs	Classroom facilities, library of books on other faiths, exchange programmes.	Professors, leaders of other religions.
Inter-faith Study Centres	Seminars, exposure programmes, living together with people of other faiths.	Study centres and facilities, inter-faith library, degree and non-degree courses.	Religious leaders, study guides.
Pastors Guild	Regular inter-faith meetings, refresher courses, exposure programmes, inter-faith prayer group meetings	Study centres, inter-faith library, sermon notes on inter-faith themes.	Leaders from other religions, dialogue experts.

RESPONSE

Ineke Reinhold-Scheuermann (The Netherlands)

* Theological education starts at home. Young parents should be educated. Their behavior in daily life should mirror the way of Jesus. An example of the way in which daily life does not reflect Jesus' way is when parents say on the telephone: "Nice to hear from you. Naturally I am pleased to pick you up and go together to church." But when the phone has been laid down, they say, "That nasty old woman is pushing me again to take her to church." Belief that *deeds and words go together* comes first in theological education.

* Theological education starts with "open-minded" Bible reading. We should read not what we think is there, but rather read and listen to the story. Parents can learn this by reading the Bible closely and then by reading the same story in a children's Bible. Parents can compare the differences they find between the two stories, and between the stories in one children's Bible and another. The teacher can try with the parents to figure out what the difference is between the two ways of telling the story. Let people become aware of the moralizing that is often in children's Bibles that is not according to what is in the Bible itself. *Listen to the open end that is in the Bible story.* Let it remain open. The listeners should during their lives puzzle with the open end and puzzle out what the meaning is for themselves during their lives. They can talk about what they think it means, knowing that everybody is seeing only part of the truth.

* Theological education means that we all see different angles of the same truth. Nobody possesses the truth; *we are searching for Jesus who is the truth*. False teachers are those who proclaim that they have the truth and who add to Bible stories an end that is not in the Bible.

* A theological education network could start a project to get writers and storytellers to tell the Bible stories for children with a close reading of the text and the knowledge of how a story is told in that language.

* A theological education network could explore and determine which stories can be told to what ages of children.

(Questions should be discussed; for example: Is it possible to tell the story of Jonah, including God's final dialogue with Jonah which ends in a question mark, to four-year-olds?)

* Theological education should teach ministers and all those who work with parents and children to consider taking courses in open-ended Bible story-telling.

* Theological education programs could include special attention to the question of the language (or languages) with which we engage in the exegesis of Bible stories.

RESPONSE
Heidi Regier Kreider (USA)

Purpose of Congregational Education

Leonor provides an excellent description of the objective of congregational education—namely "to conform individuals and communities to the image of Jesus." Also helpful is her identification of formal and informal leadership training and theological education as a tool in this process. In this way the congregation becomes the measuring stick, the test of whether leadership training and theological education are successful or not: Are healthy congregations and disciples being formed as a result? One challenge that we face in North America, in light of this purpose, is that the local congregation is a reflection of society as much as it is a reflection of Jesus. Our churches increasingly include people who are overwhelmed by the busyness, the overload of information, and the many kinds of dysfunction and pain in our society. If congregational education is to shape people into the image of Christ, it must also confront the reality people bring with them. Indeed this body of Christ must be the suffering, broken body of Christ before it is the healed and resurrected body of Christ.

Educational Materials

Leonor also speaks about the lack of good, relevant teaching materials that present the whole Gospel from an Anabaptist perspective. In North America, we do have a great volume of materials available, for those churches (the majority) who use English. Unfortunately, sometimes congregations choose to use materials with poor theology rather than the quality materials of our denomination. There is also a danger, amidst the wealth of teaching resources and materials that these become a substitute for the essence of God's word. We must continue to emphasize the importance of teachers who know God personally and model faith through their life and relationships. Another problem with some of our materials is that many are still biased toward Anglo (white), middle-class, educated or rural-background ethnic Mennonites in their stories, visual illustrations and teaching materials. As our churches grow in racial and ethnic diversity, our educational materials need to reflect that, and to be relevant for all members. A positive action in this regard is the Damascus Road Project, an educational program designed to help organizations and institutions confront racism.

Methods

Leonor speaks about inadequate methods that are not challenging or creative. We too face this problem at times, especially in adult classes that rely almost exclusively on the written or spoken word in learning. We must explore more forms of "hands-on", experiential learning that challenges the whole self, not just the mind. ("Love God with all your heart, soul, strength....") Another aspect of our teaching method is that we often separate age groups from one another for Christian education. While this recognizes important developmental differences, it alone is inadequate in forming disciples and healthy congregations. In light of the fragmenting families and homes of our North American society, we also need educational settings that are intergenerational, where people learn from those who are different from themselves. A positive step in this direction is the growing number of mentor relationships between youth and adults in our congregations, as well as the worship and study resources being published by our church that combine children, youth, and adults together.

Leadership

I affirm Leonor's emphasis on shared leadership that reflects an Anabaptist view of discipleship among all members. At the same time, I believe leadership is crucial for faithful congregational education. It is important to foster more coordination between formal, nonformal and congregational leaders who nurture an Anabaptist vision. I believe we would profit from exchanges between college/seminary professors and pastors for extended periods of time during which both would have opportunity for teaching and learning.

Conclusion

I believe Leonor's goals and hopes are the same as what we hope for our North American congregational education. Central to this is the need to promote biblical knowledge, knowledge of the living God, and environments where the Scriptures are encountered in life-giving and life-transforming ways.

3

Non-formal Theological Education: The Meserete Kristos Church Experience

Bedru Hussein (Ethiopia)

One of the greatest challenges before church leaders today is balanced church growth. Many churches are strong on one area but very weak in others. For example, many churches are very strong in evangelism but are weak in bringing the new believers into the church. Other churches are strong in worship but may be weak in teaching. There are also churches which do a great job in teaching their people, but they lack love, enthusiasm and warm fellowship.

But a truly healthy church will be growing in at least the following five ways:

1. People are being saved and are being added to the church.
2. New churches are being planted.
3. Christians are growing in their spiritual maturity.
4. The church is growing in its maturity and effectiveness.
5. There is vision and effort to reach other groups and other cultures.

The question of church growth is very important because it keeps the church itself from becoming impotent, bureaucratic, institutionally fossilized, and static.

In an impotent church, people are not growing in discipleship, the health of the church is poor, there is little effective outreach to the unchurched, and the vision of the Great Commission (Matt 28:19-20) is clouded.

The purpose of this paper is to examine and present the experience of Meserete Kristos Church's (MKC) teaching ministry specifically in the dimension of non-formal theological education and to show its ripple effect.

BACKGROUND

The Meserete Kristos Church emerged out of the Mennonite Central Committee and Eastern Mennonite Mission work which began in Ethiopia in 1948. As such it is one of the oldest evangelical churches in Ethiopia.[1]

The church, besides its spiritual ministry to its members and to the general public, also used to serve its communities in areas of education, health, agriculture, relief and development in collaboration with the overseas Mennonite agencies.

In 1982, due to the former Marxist military government's nationalization action against the church, MKC lost all its institutions including its office, worship buildings, and bank accounts as well as all physical properties. Officially it no longer existed. However, beginning July 1992, thanks to the democratization process initiated by the new government, MKC has been able to repossess seven of the church buildings. The office, guest house, book stores and all its school properties remain in the hands of the government to this day.

For almost ten years the church survived and prospered underground. The persecution was a blessing in disguise. During the underground life of the church, membership grew from 5,000 to 34,000. Fourteen congregations (local churches) multiplied to 53, while church-planting centers increased from 3 to 27, and the number of full-time workers rose from 12 to 98.

Today, six years later, those numbers have more than doubled again. Such tremendous growth posed serious challenges to the church leadership. As absolutely essential to accommodating and managing such growth, the leadership introduced three important changes. These are: a) training programs for selected trainers from the church-planting centers and local churches; b) restructuring of the church administration organogram. (See Appendix 1); and c) implementation of a pastoral care structure within the church-planting centers and local churches (see the structure on pages 65-66).

Considerable progress has been made to provide basic training for nurture, but much more has to be done. Up until this time, the MKC Head Office has adopted a four-pronged strategy which is underway. It includes:

1. A "Training of Trainers Program" in which 940 trainers from church-planting centers and local congregations are given regular structured non-formal training two times a year both

---

[1] Kraybill, N. Paul, ed., *Called to be Sent* (Scottdale: Herald Press, 1964) p. 155.

at church-planting and regional centers. The total number of training centers for this purpose are 54. (See tables 1 and 2 for the number of trainees of church-planting centers).
2. A "One Year for Christ" program, each year for 40 volunteers of young people who are given six weeks of formal teaching before being sent out on assignments of church-planting centers (see curriculum, Appendix 2, and details under III.B).
3. A Bible Institute which trains 17 evangelists on a one-year certificate level and three-year associate degree level in collaboration with Eastern Mennonite University of Harrisonburg, Virginia.[2]
4. A program of scholarship assistance that is currently training 14 leaders and trainers, besides those in the Bible institute, at home and abroad in various post high school diploma and degree programs.

In light of the explosive growth of the church and the resulting demand for leadership training on every level (non-formally or formally), there is an urgent need to continue training the lay leadership twice a year for a period of 2 to 6 days each, (two for church-planting training center trainers and five for local church trainers) so that they in turn can train others within their constituencies.

MKC has so far invested a lot in the lay leadership and the ripple effect has been tremendous. As a result, many churches have been planted and quite a number of members have ended up becoming full-time workers in the local churches as well as in the church planting centers.

According to the figures in the table below, the growth in percentage between 1982 (banning of the church) and reopening 1992 is 85.3%. Growth rate in membership between 1994 and 1995 is 10% while between 1995 and 1996 is 20%. The numerical growth of these two years, 1995 and 1996, is phenomenal. The average annual growth rate during the last 14 years is 9.5%.

Based on these statistics, the projection within the next 5 years is that the number of members will be more than 150,000, church-planting centers will number 300, local churches will number 250 and Regional Centers will number 25. (See maps, Appendix 3).

---

[2]Hansen E. Carl, *Meserete Kristos Bible Institute*, 1996-1997 Catalogue (1996) pp. 2-3, 111

The following table (taken from *Annual Reports* of MKC Head Office) depicts the phenomenal growth of MKC:

S/N	Year	Members	Number of Church planting centers	Number of local churches	Center Regional	Growth %
1	1982	5,000	3	14	—	
2	1992	34,000	27	53	—	85.3
3	1994	75,724	340	110	7	18
4	1995	83,738	364	130	11	10
5	1996	104,440	296	172	15	20

MKC'S NON-FORMAL THEOLOGICAL EDUCATION PROGRAMS

MKC has two non-formal theological training programs developed during the last 14 years for the purpose of equipping and mobilizing members to evangelize others. These are the Training of the Trainers Program, and the One Year for Christ Program.

The Training of Trainers Program

This program has been a very useful tool for five important reasons: the existence of a clearly defined educational goal; the identification of a well established educational system; the introduction of a functional pastoral care ministry for the purpose of implementing the discipleship program within the structures of church-planting centers and local churches; the experience of the baptism of the Holy Spirit; and the allocation of adequate budget.

MKC'S Educational Goal. Gangel points out to his readers that a church has to have a clear-cut educational goal. Without this there will be total chaos.[3]

From the outset, the leadership of MKC has clearly coined its educational theme based on the Apostle Paul's instruction to

---

[3]Gangel, O. Kenneth, *Building Leaders for Church Education* (Chicago: Moody Press, 1981) p. 31.

Timothy: "You then, my child, be strong in the grace that is in Christ Jesus. And what you have heard from me through many witnesses *entrust to reliable men who will be able to teach others as well*" (my emphasis) (2 Tim 2:1-2). Thus, the main educational goal of MKC is to *equip members of the church for upright Christian living and ministry (service) so that they may build the church of Jesus Christ in Ethiopia and beyond.* (Eph. 4:11-16).

MKC Educational System. The educational system that is already in place for this purpose is as follows: the Education Committee of MKC (a group of 7) along with the Education Secretary and Teachers Council, all together 12 at the Head Office level, meet 6 times in a year. The Council selects relevant subjects most of the time dwelling on felt needs of the church. (See MKC organogram, Appendix 1). Once the selection is done, assignments are given to individuals or to a team of two or three members to prepare the teaching materials. Usually two materials are prepared at a time. Eventually, the council of twelve teachers breaks into two groups. Then the council comes together on a fixed date to go through the materials to edit theological and grammatical errors. In the process of editing a learning situation takes place. And later each Council member will be given a copy to make a self-study on the material. Meanwhile, the two materials will be typed and duplicated and kept until the next training program commences.

Usually in the first month of the Ethiopian New Year (September), the Education Committee fixes teaching months and dates and notifies the selected trainees of the local churches. On the date of the training program trainees will come to the strategically located centers from their local churches where the assigned teachers go, taking the prepared materials with them. The trainers make sure that they have with them enough copies and attendance sheets. The teaching program will then take place as scheduled.

With regard to trainees, selection is done upon the recommendation of the local churches and church-planting centers based on the selection criteria produced by the Education Committee. Some of the criteria are maturity in Christian life, Bible knowledge, ability to communicate the truth, preferably pedagogical exposure and teaching experience (Teachers' Training Institution graduates have this experience.)

This training program takes place twice a year for a period of 6 days. So far there are 20 selected centers and five more will be added in the 1996-97 fiscal year training period. Evaluation is done by giving written examinations to the trainees. The examination papers are corrected and grades are collected on a roster. At the end of the year, prizes are awarded to trainees who stand in the top three places. This exercise has encouraged and motivated them to study the materials they are given.

Fremont and Sara Regier in their Research Project on African Non-formal Theological Education Programs strongly note that students testify to the empowerment received through their TEE (Theological Education by Extension) in African countries.[4] MKC trainees also witness that the training they are receiving has given them new insights and is providing them with sharp tools for ministry.

TABLE 1
Indicates the training centers, number of trainees of local churches and the medium of instruction:

S/N	Training Center	Number of Trainees	Medium of Instruction
1	Addis Ababa	42	Amharic
2	Nazareth	33	Amharic
3	Metehara	12	Amharic
4	Dire Dawa	23	Amharic
5*	Agamssa	42	Oromifa
6*	Gelila	47	"
7*	Dengeb	43	"
8*	Meta Robi	33	"
9*	Nazareth	15	"
10*	Gindeberet	13	"

---

[4]Regier, Fremont and Sara, *African Non-formal Theological Education Research Project* (ANTERP), (North Newton, Kansas, 1994) p. 20.

S/N	Training Center	Number of Trainees	Medium of Instruction
11*	Gimbi	13	"
12*	Nekempte	13	"
13*	Shambu	30	"
14*	Aje	10	"
15*	Adamitulu	12	"
16*	Meki	15	"
17*	Mojo	15	"
18*	Kone	13	"
19*	Uka	10	"
20*	Tiya	13	"
	TOTAL NUMBER	447	

TABLE 2

The New Training Centers and number of trainees planned for February and July 1997 are the following. See Table below:

S/N	Training Center	Number of Trainees	Medium of Instruction
1	Zewaye	20	Amharic
2	Shone	20	Amharic
3	Hassaena	20	Amharic
4	Bahir Dar	20	Amharic
5	Welliso	20	Amharic
	TOTAL	100	

The grand total of tables 1 and 2 is 547 (All names of Centers and figures are taken from the Education Department of the MKC).

Trainees of Centers 5*-20* come from Oromo-speaking congregations. The Amharic materials are translated into Oromo language for training and teaching purposes as well.

The titles of training covered during the September 1996-July 1997 year as a sample are the following: I Corinthians (book study), Haggai (book study), the Cross, Worship. (For further information, see training areas covered within the last 13 years, Appendix 4).

As already indicated, those who have taken this training will go to their local churches and teach others so that they in turn can teach members within the structure of the pastoral care ministry.

The church-planting center trainers are also trained in the same pattern. Thus, 393 trainees attend 29 strategically located centers to get the two-day training, then return to train others. (See curriculum, Appendix 4).

Pastoral Care Ministry. The Pastoral Care Ministry has been patterned after the example set forth by Christ in his ministry on earth. Jesus was very much involved with his disciples in a "small group" setting, as well as being present ministering to the multitudes. Acts 2 describes a two-pronged pattern for believers, gathering in large-group meetings and in small cell groups.

Rather than competing, each format provided essential elements to the growth of the believers. The home cell group (care groups) provided nurturing (teaching), fellowship, prayer, and outreach opportunities.

In the New Testament we see that home gatherings were held at the homes of Priscilla and Aquila (Rom. 16), Nympha (Col. 4:15) and Philemon. These home gatherings completed the meetings held in the temple and the synagogues, providing expression of church family life.

Historically, a reinstitution of the use of small groups has accompanied almost every recorded revival. Many say that John Wesley's eighteenth-century revival flourished because he organized the converts into groups of ten, each with its own leader. The famous "haystack prayer meetings" grew out of a group who met regularly to pray for the spiritual welfare of their fellow students. The meetings led to the first student missionary society in

America which provided the main impulse for the foreign missionary movement of American churches.[5]

The Yoido Full Gospel Church of Seoul, Korea, led by David Yonggi Cho, has a similar experience of providing a pastoral care ministry to the members of the church. Pastor Cho started a home cell unit system for the purpose of nurture, prayer, and fellowship. Today, the church has more than 50,000 home cells[6] and more than 700,000 members. This network is the mainstream for the life of the church.[7]

Meserete Kristos Church introduced pastoral care ministry in 1980 prior to its underground church life. Due to the severity of the persecution, a careful study of establishing a pastoral care ministry through home cell networks was necessitated. As a result, the ministry was refined and fully introduced into local church and church-planting center settings.

Included with the following summary of the functions of the pastoral care committee is a chart which represents the pastoral care structure of the local church. The chart shows a superimposed pastoral care structure, a practical tool for the discipleship training of members in cell groups.

Functions of the Pastoral Care Committee
1. Responsible to the elders.
2. Elected on the basis of their gifts by the elders.
3. Facilitate training programs (nurture) for members of different groups (older members, new converts, and children) through the pastoral sub-committee in their respective home-cell groups.
4. Coordinate the activities of different committees (Great Commission, Youth Committee, etc.) give periodic reports to elders.
5. Hear periodic reports from pastoral sub-committees and give general guidelines if needed.
6. Carry out additional duties assigned by elders.

---

[5]Tuttle G. Robert, *John Wesley, His Life and Theology* (Grand Rapids: Francis Asbury Press, 1978) pp. 135-137.
[6]Kannadey, Peggy, ed., *Church Growth Magazine* (Autumn 1992) p. 13.
[7]Cho, Yonggi David, ed. *Ibid.* (Autumn 1995) p. 5.

THEOLOGICAL EDUCATION ON FIVE CONTINENTS

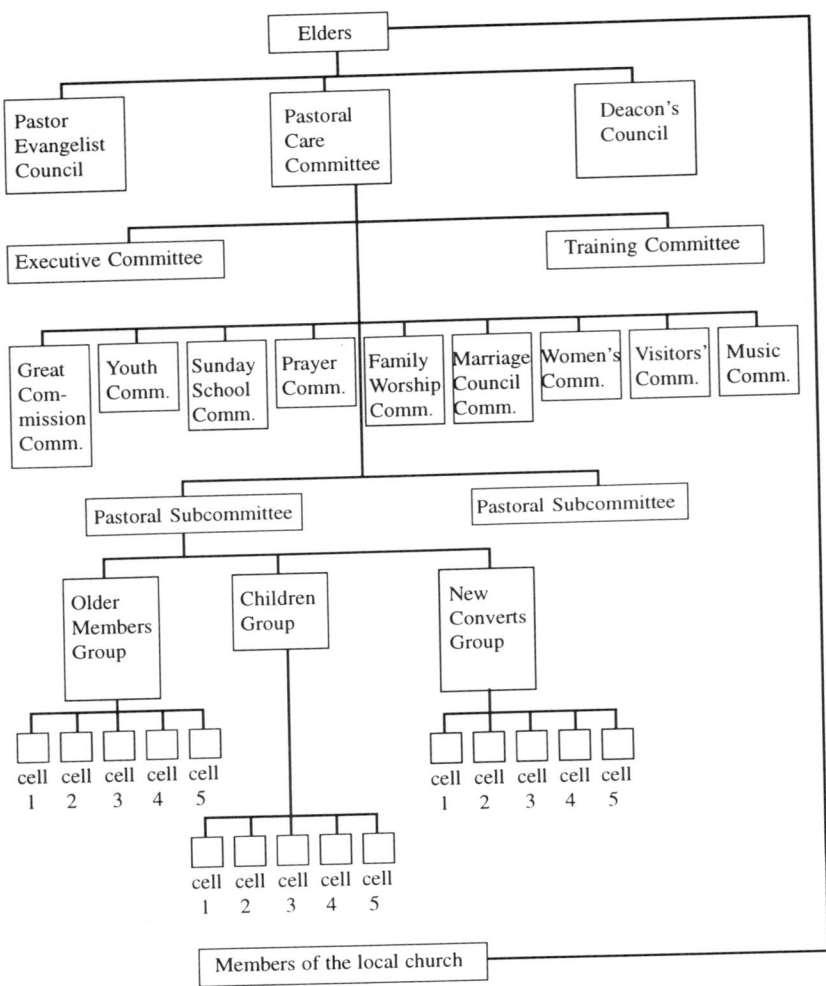

Pastoral Sub-Committee
1. Responsible to the pastoral-care committee.
2. Elected by the elders council on the basis of their gifts.
3. Keep records of members of its constituency (sex, age, date of new birth experience, date of water baptism, marital status, level of education, etc.)

4. Organize cell groups in accordance to their level of maturity together with necessary follow up.
5. Use the teaching materials prepared by the main education committee (at the head office level) indicated in the curriculum for different levels of maturity (see the curriculum, Appendix 4).
6. Evaluate the activities of home cell groups along with the cell group leaders.
7. Organize cell groups for new converts and follow through until baptism and into the next stage of training.
8. Carry out additional duties assigned by the pastoral care committee.

The experience of the baptism of the Holy Spirit. Another factor which is responsible for the existence of a strong and ongoing discipleship program in MKC is the belief and experience of the baptism of the Holy Spirit—the dynamite promise. This experience has birthed biblical power and biblical patterns. As a result, MKC church leaders teach members about the baptism of the Holy Spirit in the local church-planting centers, and members are observed to experience the dynamite power from the Holy Spirit according to Act 1:8.

The promise of power from God is that God will equip the saints based upon his authority to make disciples. God will equip members to do his work, be his regents and see his Kingdom built everywhere among tribes of Ethiopia and other nations as well (Matt 28:19-20, Luke 24:49). Accordingly, MKC's immediate and future goal is to reach the different tribes of Ethiopia and to go out to other nations of the world. Meanwhile, MKC also seeks to motivate and encourage Ethiopian Christians in the diaspora to reach peoples in the different cultures where they are currently living.

Budget Allocation. After having seen the ripple effect of the educational program of the head office of MKC, the leadership has been allocating an educational budget every year.

The following table shows the MKC head office budget allocation for nine sections and departments. (All figures taken from Annual Budget of MKC head office. Currency is in Ethiopian Birr [1 USD - 6.35 Birr]. *Includes literature, pension, and Regional Centers Coordination Department)

S/N	Budget fiscal year Eth. C.	Total budget for the year	Admin. Dept.	Education Dept.	Bible Institute	Pastoral Care Dept.	Evan & Church Dept.	Development Dept.	Other* Depts.
1	1985	529,000	147,739	86,253	—	92,930	156,887	15,992	29,199
2	1986	1,043,475	265,568	212,816	—	124,059	174,814	42,899	223,309
3	1987	1,308,322	254,855	336,141	—	191,787	251,301	65,796	226,442
4	1988	1,445,312	373,107	274,775	117,920	207,836	255,295	78,579	137,799
5	1989	1,592,713	358,073	404,309	156,335	191,445	160,567	67,335	254,649

The two departments that deal directly with non-formal training programs are the Education and Evangelism Church Planting Departments. Both have an average of 39.3% budget allocation when compared to other sections and departments. This shows that a high priority is given to non-formal training programs.

One Year for Christ Non-formal Training Program

The One Year for Christ is a unique discipleship non-formal training program of MKC focused on bringing young adults into a more intimate relationship with Jesus Christ and equipping them to serve others and make disciples out in the church-planting centers. This program has strong similarities with Youth Evangelism Service (YES) program of Eastern Mennonite Mission of Salunga, Pennsylvania.

The One Year for Christ program was started in the 1970s with the vision that young men after having two weeks of training would be placed in local churches without full-time workers.

Later, in the 1980s, the program was evaluated and the need for having young men in the field, especially in church-planting centers, was identified. Consequently the term of service was raised to one full year program and the training was also expanded from 2 weeks to 6 weeks. To this effect, a training curriculum was designed (See Appendix 2).

This exercise has brought about effective and encouraging results. Furthermore, the program has served as a screening test for those who would like to enter full-time ministry. So far, more than 200 young men have participated and 30% of them have ended up becoming full-time workers.

Non-Formal Theological Education

The following processes take place to recruit, equip and send young people to local churches and church planting centers:
1. Select 40 dedicated young men for the program based upon local church recommendations. (An interview is given to each candidate by the facilitators of the program.)
2. Identify and assign teachers to give the training (months of November and January).
3. Train for 6 weeks using the curriculum designed for the program at the MKC Bible Institute.
4. Issue pertinent handouts, books, and other materials for each course to the trainees.
5. Give evaluatory examinations at the end of each course.
6. Graduate the trainees upon successful completion.
7. Issue a certificate along with the transcript.
8. Assign to church-planting centers and local churches.
9. Supervise (oversee) the work through the personnel of the head office of the Evangelism and Church Planting Department.

OUTSTANDING RESULTS OF NON-FORMAL THEOLOGICAL EDUCATION

MKC has been experiencing growth in many aspects due to the implementation of a continuous and timely educational program all the way down the line of its church structure. The following are the indicators of growth in the local churches as well as in the church planting centers as observed in MKC's experience.

Spiritual Growth
Progress in spiritual growth cannot be made without accompanying growth in the spiritual lives of members of the church. Although spiritual growth is more difficult to measure, there are many indications of this growth observable within the MKC.

One clear indication of spiritual growth is that the members have learned to pray with expectancy and love to pray. Prayer meetings are held in some local churches every morning and evening. There are prayer groups that meet in private homes. All-night prayer is also made every month in most local churches and church-planting centers. Furthermore, prayer is a prominent part of Sunday services and cell group meetings. People also come to church buildings during the day to pray. All of these prayers build up the members and their relationship with the Lord.

Prayers are often accompanied by fasting. The length varies depending on the nature of the issue to be prayed upon. Generally, there is a strong emphasis on prayer whether individually, corporately or in some type of small group setting.

The members in the church are also strongly discipled in many areas of Christian life and ministry. As already indicated, the teaching materials used are the materials produced by the head office education committee. The teachers are those trained by the trainers who themselves got the training from the head office teaching team. In fact, local churches use curriculum designed by the pastoral committee of the head office and they know what to teach to the different groups they have in their churches.

Organic Growth

Singletary points out that organic growth involves the leadership and shepherding network of a church. When defining organic growth he says that it pertains to the infrastructure or cellular growth within churches. It consists of all sorts of subgroups, small groups, and networks so vital to the assimilation, nurture and mobilization of the membership.[8]

The experience of MKC fits Singletary's explanation. Due to the continuous process of discipleship activities, the church has a high level of lay mobilization, that is, a relatively small percentage of the membership are spectators. There is also numerical growth which in turn results in healthy mitosis (cell division) or reproduction of local churches, for example when a larger cell group breaks into four, as in the case of the Dire Dawa local church. (See case study A, below.) Furthermore, new areas are evangelized by the members and church-planting centers are eventually initiated.

Numerical Growth

Numerical growth, defined as a growth in the number of believers in the local churches, is one of the most important ways in which a church can grow. It is quite clear from the biblical point of view that God wants the church to grow numerically. God wants churches to make disciples of all nations (Matt 28:19) and is not

---

[8]Wagner, Arn Towns, ed., *Church Growth State of Art*, (Wheaton: Tyndale House, 1989) p. 114.

Non-Formal Theological Education

willing that any should perish (2 Pet 3:9). An example of continually adding people to the church is clearly seen in early church history (Acts 2:47).

In the experience of the Meserete Kristos Church, numerical growth is quite evident due to its intensive educational program carried out within local churches and church planting centers, as noted in the following case studies.

The Nazareth Meserete Kristos Local Churches. The Nazareth Meserete Kristos churches are geographically located in Nazareth town, 100 kilometers southeast of Addis Ababa, the capital city of Ethiopia. This is the town where Eastern Mennonite Mission began its work. Prior to that, in 1948, Mennonite Relief Committee of Elkhart, Inc., sent workers to do relief and rehabilitation work.[9] Up until 1982 there has been this local church whose membership was not more than 300.

The leadership using the training materials produced by the education committee of MKC continued to disciple the members. Eventually, the pastoral care ministry was introduced. Home cell groups were formed and the work continued up until 1992. Due to the numerical growth of the church, there was a need to divide the church into two local churches. In accordance with the Meserete Kristos Church Constitution, Article 5 number 2.*[10] The necessary preparations were then made and in 1992, the local church was divided into two.

Two years later, due to the expansion of the work and numerical growth within the two local churches of Nazareth, they underwent a second division. As a result, they became four local churches. These churches are the Semen (North), Misrak (East), Debub (South) and Mierab (West) Nazareth Meserete Kristos Churches. The four churches are located in four different sections of the town, run and administered by their own elders. After restructuring themselves, they have their own pastors and evangelists, worship places, and home cell groups and still have an intact pastoral care ministry which caters to the nurture of their members. Furthermore, the four local churches of Nazareth have their own outreach centers where churches are planted. According to the annual report of the Nazareth regional center of August 1996,

---

[9]Kraybill, p. 114.
[10]MKC Head Office, *MKC Constitution, Part II*, Article 5 number 2, p. 19.

the membership in the four local churches is: Semen - 1003, Misrak - 1021, Debub - 716 and Mierab - 722, totalling 3472. (See table below).

The following table shows the key factors that are responsible for growth in the case of Nazareth churches.

S/N	VARIOUS GROUPS	SEMEN (NORTH)	MISRAK (EAST)	DEBUB (SOUTH)	MIERAB (WEST)
1	Total membership	1003	1021	726	722
2	No. of pastoral care committees	1	1	1	1
	Total no. involved	9	9	10	9
3	No. of sub-pastoral committee group	2	2	2	2
	Total no. involved	18	18	12	12
4	No. of trainers cell group	12	10	7	7
	Total no. involved	173	158	140	111
5	No. of older church cell group	15	17	21	16
	Total no. involved	370	323	420	324
6	No. of new member cell group	10	8	9	7
	Total no. involved	358	133	68	100
7	No. of cell children's group	15	19	12	10
	Total no. involved	356	260	177	110
8	No. of cell prayer group	16	26	15	19
	Total no. involved	219	244	232	174
9	No. of church planting centers	4	1	2	2

As indicated in the table, four of the local churches have 2 sub-pastoral committees. If they continue giving the training using the curriculum for the next 3 years, there is no doubt that all of them will become local churches. Therefore, in Nazareth town itself, there will be 8 local churches in place. This will be true for Dire Dawa as well.

The number of cell groups in each local church is also something worth noting. Observing the table above, each local church has the following: Semen - 68, Misrak - 80, Debub - 64, and Mirab - 59 for a current total of 271 living cells.

Dire Dawa Meserete Kristos Local Church. Dire Dawa is another local church of Meserete Kristos Church which is located in the Eastern part of Ethiopia, 520 kilometers away from Addis Ababa. Dire Dawa was also originally started by Mennonite Mission.

Until 1982, it was one local church and the membership was not more than 200. In 1993, the Dire Dawa church introduced the pastoral care ministry and started with one pastoral care committee and with four sub-pastoral units. This means that the whole local church was organized in four groups based on their geographical locations in the town. Educational programs were then organized and given to different groups (home cell groups) of members using the curriculum. A year later, the four sub-pastoral units were promoted to local church level. To date, the four local churches have reorganized themselves by establishing pastoral care structure and subsequently experiencing spiritual, organic, numerical and outreach (mission) growth. The total membership of the four local churches as reported in August 1996 is Kezira - 703, Megalla - 584, Merab - 752 and Misrak - 635, for a total of 2670.[11]

Church Planting

One outstanding strength of MKC is planting new churches aggressively. Within the first 14 years it has grown from 14 local congregations to 172, and from 3 church-planting centers to 296 church-planting centers.

Historically, MKC worked only in the eastern part of the country. This demarcation was made by mission agencies some 35 years ago. Each mainline denomination had their own geographical boundaries of mission and church activities. Today, this boundary is overrun by the work of the Holy Spirit. As a result, MKC is everywhere in the country. (See Appendix 3).

---

[11]Nazareth Regional Center (MKC) *Annual Report* (August 1996).

Foltz and Henry remind their readers that the church exists for mission. To this effect, all church departments are to result in the furthering of the mission.[12]

Accordingly, MKC has a high priority on evangelism. The different activities like conferences (mini-crusades), outreaches (Great Commission Committees activities) and altar calls all contribute to church growth. Every Sunday, many respond, coming forward for prayer and further instructions. During these occasions, members, especially women, give the traditional crackling sound called "ililta" and cheer—an expression of joy and praise to the Lord when persons come forward to accept the Lord Jesus Christ. This momentous event demonstrates that the heart of the members of the church is set on "evangelizing the lost."

Most of MKC's local churches and church-planting centers have their structures suited for reaching unreached peoples as well. For instance, the Jimma MKC local church, located in the southwest of the country, is reaching the Kaffa and Menja tribes. The Gambella MKC local church, located in the western part of the country, is reaching the tribes of Agnuwak and Gambella. The Dengebe local church, located, close to the Sudan border, is reaching the Shinasha tribe. The Kibremengist, a church-planting center of Shakiso local church, located in the southern part of the country, is reaching the Guji tribe. The presence of local churches and church-planting centers will sooner or later affect the people in the area.

Church-planting center Case Study - Bahir Dar. Bahir Dar is a regional government town located in the northwest of Ethiopia, 565 kilometers away from Addis Ababa. It has a population of 127,000. Church work started in 1988 with three members of MKC who went to this place because of government jobs.

MKC head office, through its evangelism and church planting department, started training programs for the three members together with five other members coming from the surrounding towns. Over six years there was continual growth in membership. As a result, Bahir Dar was considered as one of the MKC's church-planting centers. Due to the introduction of the pastoral care ministry, numerical, spiritual, and organic growth were observed. Furthermore, the center even went out to reach other

---

[12]Foltz, L. Howard & Henry Mark. *Triumph Missions Renewal for the Local Church*, (Joplin: Messenger Publishing House, 1994) p. 108.

neighboring towns and established other church-planting centers. In 1994, because there were enough people that could be leaders and the group was self-supporting, it was promoted to a local church status.

To date, Bahir Dar has 315 members, 17 church-planting centers, three evangelists and two One Year for Christ workers. In fact, the local church has one student studying for his first degree in one of the theological colleges in the country.[13] Furthermore, in its pastoral care structure the local church has two sub-pastoral care committees and 70 home cell groups. This local church is now intensively using the training curriculum and is expecting to divide into two local churches probably within the next two years.

In Bahir Dar, there are three secular training institutions. A lot of work (mostly discipleship and follow up) is done to evangelize the students of these institutions. As a result, every year 10-15 Christian students graduate and are assigned to different places of the country. These graduates in turn become church planters. This is true for most Christian students, who graduate from other higher institutions in the country as well.

Church Structure

Smith says that complex doctrines and structures may be useful for theological classification and church management, but they do little to move hearts towards conversion. He further says that unless the church relates all doctrines and structures to the goal of proclaiming the simple message of the gospel, these doctrines and structures will have little impact on people's lives.[14]

MKC leadership concurs. As a result, it has so far maintained structures that are conducive to evangelism. Depending on the need, structures have been continually changed to suit both management and educational programs.

In MKC experience, a new structure was developed in 1992 to accommodate and manage the fast growing number of churches. This new structure brought decentralization of authority and activities to the regions, (See church organogram, Appendix 1).

The existing structure also shows that each region will have its own education committee. The main duty of this committee is to

---

[13]Bahir Dar MKC Local Church, *Annual Report* (August 1996).
[14]Smith, C. Glenn, ed., *Evangelizing Adults* (Wheaton: Tyndale House, 1985) p. 67.

coordinate all educational programs of the region in collaboration with the education department of the MKC head office. Every time a new region is established, there will be a regional training center in place in order to facilitate the educational program.

The other structure that keeps the training program always in motion is the pastoral care structure, an integral part of a local church and church-planting center. It is always there to cater to the feeding or nurturing of members of the church. Beyond any shadow of doubt, a structure of this nature with people being motivated, involved, and operating in it is very important to any growing church.

Lay Mobilization

Every believer has a part in Christ's ministry. In fact, Paul frequently associates "the ministry" with the work of all of God's people. He said, "We are putting no obstacle in anyone's way, so that no fault may be found with our ministry, but as servants of God we have commended ourselves in every way" (2 Cor. 6:3-4). To the Ephesians, Paul wrote: "to equip the saints for ministry, for building up the body of Christ, until all of us come to the unity of the faith and of the knowledge of the Son of God, to maturity, to the measure of the full stature of Christ" (Eph .4:12-13).

Clearly there is a ministry to which Christ's body is called. Churches have to mobilize lay people into the ministry by recruiting, training, and assigning them to do the work in the areas of their gifts.

Kennedy warns that one of the greatest victories Satan has ever scored is the idea which he has foisted off on probably 90 percent of the Christian church that it is the task of full-time ministers, pastors, and evangelists only to share the gospel of Christ and that this is not the job of lay people. He adds that Satan has been so successful with this stratagem that it has been estimated that probably 95 percent of his own church members never lead anyone to Christ.[15]

According to the experience of MKC, there is a high level of lay mobilization in all local churches and church-planting centers. As much as possible members are assigned in home cell groups for discipleship programs and according to their gifts members are requested to serve within the structure. As a result, many members

---

[15]Smith, C. Glenn, pp. 37-40.

of MKC due to the solid leadership training they get through its educational system are serving not only MKC but also other evangelical churches. For instance, there are many members of MKC who are chosen to be leaders in various committees that deal with evangelical churches fellowships, para-church organizations and student fellowships. In most cases the members are lay leaders, not full-time workers.

CONCLUSION

Running a big country-wide educational program has not been carried out without problems, such as financial constraints and dropouts of trainees. Sometimes trainers from the head office and trainees as well are forced to take their annual leave to do the work. In some centers, trainees may not arrive on time due to transportation problems. Therefore, the training continues until midnight, putting pressure and inconvenience on both the trainers and the trainees themselves and to some extent affecting the learning-teaching process.

With the ever increasing number of churches and church-planting centers, administration in non-formal theological education must be constantly growing. It takes all the wisdom, skill, and Christlikeness one can bring to the task. To this end, the spearheading education committee members and the teachers' council of MKC are sacrificing their family time, social life, and convenience. This is also true to some extent of the trainers in the local churches and church-planting centers—a major weak point that should be addressed by the leadership.

Although the work demands sacrifice on all sides, the Meserete Kristos Church through its timely functioning non-formal theological education program has experienced a growing life of worship, fellowship, and evangelism among its members in almost all its constituencies. This is evidenced by the organic and annual numerical growth of the regional centers, local churches, church-planting centers and membership.

In order to accommodate such growth and expansion and to reflect the message of Jesus Christ, the administrative as well as the educational structures (the pastoral care structure) are continuously restructured. This exercise has enabled MKC to produce leaders and mobilize the laity in various disciplines of church ministries.

Therefore, if MKC continues with this trend for the next five years it will reach many unreached areas of Ethiopia and will have mission work started elsewhere outside the country consequently fulfilling the Great Commission (Matt 28:19).

Appendix 1

MKC Organogram

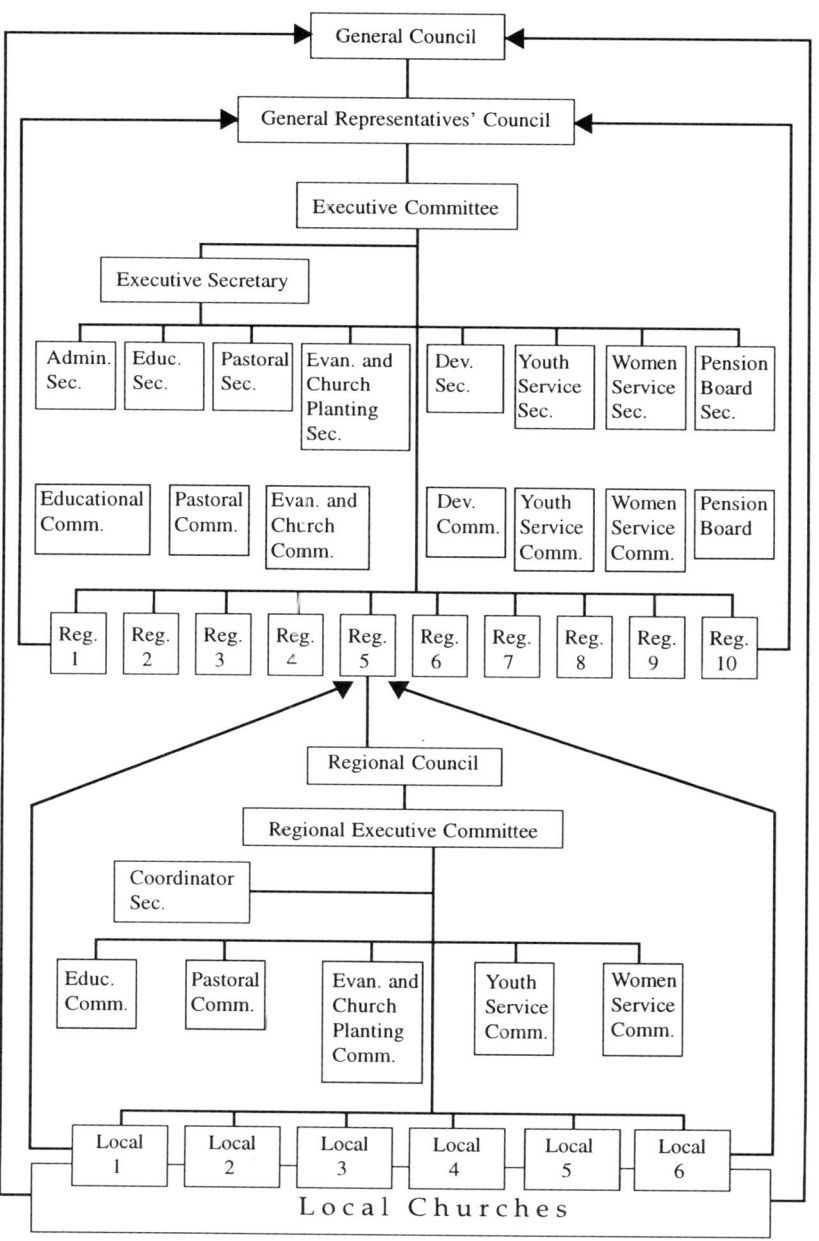

APPENDIX 2

ONE YEAR FOR CHRIST – TRAINING COURSES

S/No.	SUBJECT/TITLE	HOURS
1	MKC Church Doctrine	20
2	How to Preach/Methodology	20
3	Old Testament Survey	30
4	New Testament Survey	30
5	Gifts and Fruits of the Holy Spirit	20
6	Master Life (discipleship)	20
7	Hermeneutics	30
8	Evangelism and Church Planting	20

Appendix 3

Meserete Kristos Church before 1982
(Nationalization)
Distribution of Local Churches
Map A

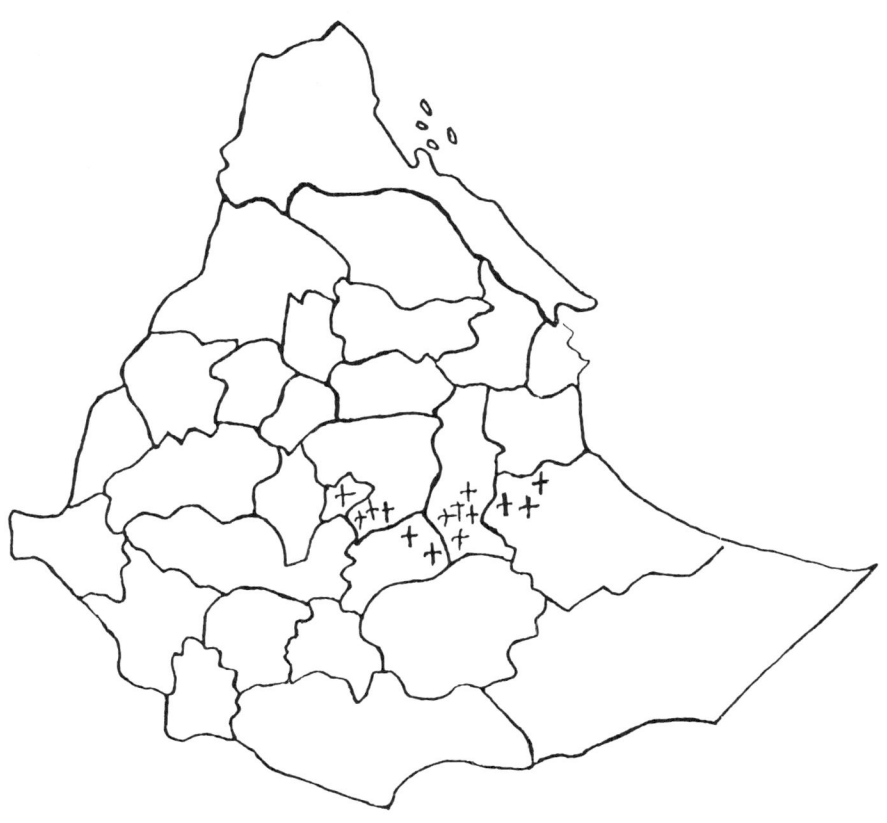

Key:
+ = Local churches -----------------14
() = Church planting centers ----NIL
∇ = ---------------------------------NIL

Appendix 4

Meserete Kristos Church Today
(1996)
Distribution of Local Churches and
Church Planting Centers

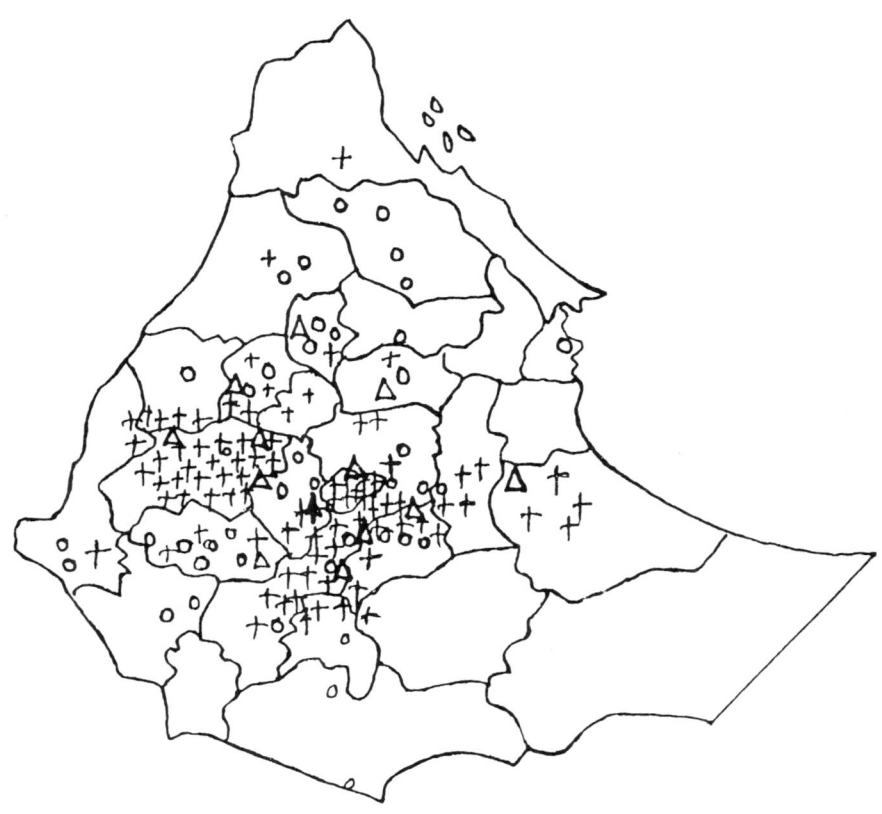

Key:
+ = Local churches--------------- 172
() = Church planting centers ---- 296
∇ = ---------------------------------45

APPENDIX 5

MKC Non-formal Theological Training Curriculum

A. New Members
   1. Following Jesus (Chapters 1-3)
   2. Water Baptism

B. Older Members
   3. Following Jesus (Chapters 4-6)
   4. Holy Communion
   5. Forgiveness
   6. Following Jesus (Chapters 7-8)
   7. The church
   8. Following Jesus (Chapters 9-10)
   9. Spiritual Authority (Chapters 1-2)
   10. MKC Statement of Faith
   11. Book Study - Ephesians
   12. Character study - Abraham
   13. Stewardship (Finance)

C. Trainers/Leaders
   14. Book Study - I Peter
   15. Divine Guidance
   16. Atonement
   17. Spiritual Man
   18. Spiritual Authority (Chapters 3 - 18)
   19. The Holy Spirit
   20. Bible Study methods
   21. How to lead Bible study groups
   22. Organizing Bible study groups
   23. Preaching
   24. New Testament survey
   25. Old Testament survey
   26. Sunday School/Methodology
   27. Planning and Organizing

RESPONSE
Wendy Binks (India)

It has been interesting to read through and think about this paper and somewhat of a challenge to write a reply. The whole concept of the MKC experience is completely outside of anything I have ever known or thought about. My concept of non-formal theological education borders on the informal. However, I am in total agreement with the opening statement: "One of the greatest challenges before church leaders today is balanced church growth." The fourth paragraph is also highly relevant to my situation: "In an impotent church, people aren't growing in discipleship, the health of the church is poor, there is little effective outreach to the unchurched, and the vision of the Great Commission is clouded." The churches with which I work are decidedly impotent, with witchcraft, alcoholism and immorality on the increase.

I admire the organization that MKC has set up to deal with the challenges coming from the incredible growth of MKC. Obviously laity have had to take a much more active role than in many churches and thus must be a tremendous strength of the church today. I know that some of the churches with which I work do have such organizational structures but I have yet to see any real benefit from this. The Christian community in our area is large but mainly spectator-based. The priests are disheartened. The programs to train lay people seem superficial, with no lasting visible effect. I have come into my situation from an international, inter-denominational mission and work with another interdenominational organization (TAFTEE–The Association for Theological Education by Extension) which, although Indian, is a member of yet another international organization, (SEAN–Seminary by Extension to all Nations). We offer Theological Education by Extension (TEE) in most of the major Indian languages at certificate level; at degree level in English, with translation going on into two main Indian languages (I am coordinating the translation into Hindi), and a masters course in English which is affiliated with Oxford University in England. Like MKC our theme is from 2 Timothy 2.2: "Entrust to faithful people who will be able to teach others as well," and the educational goal from Ephesians 4:12 "to equip members of the church for an upright Christian living and ministry so that they may build the church of Jesus Christ." The problem I face is that the supposedly "faithful people" do not see any need to learn.

For many years the Bihar Mennonite Mandli (BMM) had not sent anyone for training. Now all the pastors are getting very old and they have suddenly realized that they have no leadership in training. The two candidates sent to Bible school have now returned and are not at all suitable for the needs of the church. One young man and one woman who is in poor health are now in training; one woman was trained and began to work well but has since married and gone elsewhere. In this situation some local men have now been chosen who have shown some willingness to lead their churches but for family, economic, and educational reasons are not able to go away for training. I was asked to use the certificate level course to train these men, amongst others, in basic pastoral theology, and the men know that they will be eligible for ordination upon completion of the course. However, the course requirement of a weekly discussion group has been a stumbling block as they try to study with all the distractions of a busy life and their church work. It is also difficult to find enough literate people in each area to form a group. The men do not seem entirely convinced that they need training and do not give priority to their studies. We now have the situation in one church where the men who form the church committee are too drunk or lethargic to take the Sunday service, and so sometimes young girls who have studied the course are suddenly faced with taking the service and preaching with only five minutes notice—and are capable of doing so! The difference between BMM and MKC as portrayed in Bedru Hussein's paper is so enormous that there is no comparison.

In Appendix 2 I was a little surprised to see so much emphasis on the Holy Spirit (20 hours) and no specific teaching on God the Father or the life and work of our Lord Jesus Christ. I wonder if this leads to an unbalanced approach to what the young people teach when they go to their church-planting centers. It was helpful to see the map in Appendix 4. It was good to see a central core of churches and work spreading out from them. With such an emphasis on church planting I was surprised to see a group of churches, along with a regional center, in the east with no church planting center close by. Also there seem to be some very isolated church planting centers with no nearby church which must make for a lonely situation for those involved in church planting. There was no mention in the paper of any particular regular meetings for people in such situations apart from the ongoing training sessions. I wonder if people in the church-planting centers have regular pastoral visits from the regional centers. Having had experience of working in an isolated situation for many years, I know just how important, and how difficult, it is for regular visits to be made, not just for administrative purposes but also for pastoral care. The ripple effect of non-formal theological education is difficult to assess. Obviously in this very structured set-up of MKC immediate results are more obvious.

I have been encouraged by some of my students' ability now to evaluate teaching and, on occasions, stand up in a meeting to correct false teaching that occasionally comes from the variety of traveling preachers who descend on unwary congregations. Their understanding has led to changes in attitudes as they go about their daily work in such a way that causes comments from colleagues both Christian and non-Christian. One unlooked for result of non-formal TE that I have found is an acceptance and increased understanding of other denominations so that, at least on an individual basis, there is increased tolerance and a willingness to work with people from other denominations. I am wondering what the situation is in Ethiopia. Brother Bedru has mentioned that, historically, mission agencies made a demarcation with each denomination having geographical boundaries and mentions that now MKC is everywhere in the country. Has there been any interdenominational discussion about this? Is the main point of TE to bring people to a fuller knowledge of the Bible and to follow our Lord Jesus more closely, or to bring them into a closer affiliation with one particular denomination? In an area where "sheep stealing" is very common and leads to a lot of ill feeling, I have had to be very careful to emphasize that the course I introduce is to strengthen the church, no matter what denomination and that I expect students to remain in their own church and use their training to strengthen that particular church.

An aspect of non-formal TE that interests me, although I have no experience and it is not at all mentioned in this paper, is *how to make non-formal TE accessible to illiterate people.* I am trying to get some of my students and group leaders to write songs that incorporate the basic theology that they teach so that illiterate people can easily remember and teach others. In a church that has at least 25 percent illiterate membership, this could be important. There is also opportunity to teach non-formal TE to the large nominal Christian population that inhabits our local jails, but we lack the "faithful people" to implement this program.

RESPONSE
José Gallardo (Spain)

Introduction

It is difficult to translate what is happening in the Meserete Kristos Church experience to the context of Spain or Europe at large. Nevertheless there is a challenging testimony of the power of God and the readiness of a faithful people to serve Him. It is also an example of how the negative and evil circumstances under the Marxist regime worked for the good of the church, bringing maturity and growth.

No doubt, our Ethiopian brothers and sisters were the first to be surprised by what God was doing and overwhelmed by the results of those years of hardship. It is true that they had prepared the way for the Lord and they deserve some of the credit. They deserve credit for their good adaptation during the years of persecution and also for their capacity to answer the emerging new reality of a rapidly growing church so that it continued to grow and gave the new members the attention and formation they needed.

Many times, in some movements, when there is growth in numbers there is also growth in superficiality and passivity. Or even, many of those who join quickly, very soon leave in the same way because of lack of care and training that would help them give what they received.

What is helpful in the presentation of Bedru Hussein for my work

In my ministry, I have two main areas of work. One is as an itinerant preacher and teacher going to different churches and conferences in Europe, mostly in France, among Mennonites, and in Spain, among churches of various denominations which have experienced a charismatic renewal. The other area is planting new churches, evangelizing, discipling, and helping new congregations to train their young leaders as well as overseeing a ministry among drug addicts, delinquents, prisoners, outcasts, and persons with AIDS in the terminal stage of their lives.

Even though what is happening in the MKC defies my imagination and even my faith, when I consider Europe I learn many lessons. It is true that nothing similar is actually happening in

Europe among Mennonites, and I tend to think that it will never happen. But that is the first lesson, one of faith and hope. Why could something similar not happen to us? Is God less powerful in Europe? Is our materialism, intellectualism, and religious indifference a greater problem than the poverty, ignorance, and animism of Africa? Are they more in need of God than we are? Is our social comfort and secularism an impossible barrier? Will we have this situation forever?

Sometimes I wonder if what happened to the former Yugoslavia cannot happen to Spain with the different nationalisms and the terrorism of E.T.A., the Basque separatist movement. But is it only through suffering and persecution that God can draw the human race closer and bring about revival in our midst?

Besides the lessons of faith and hope for a greater harvest in our dry land I also learn about the need for programs, structure, and organization, the concept of the church and the priesthood of all believers, and the role of the Holy Spirit.

In our European context, probably as part of our colonial bias, most of the time there is a concept about African people being informal and disorganized. Maybe the images of chaos we watched on TV in the past months about Zaire and Rwanda have impressed in our minds the idea of disorder, irrationality, and extremism of all kinds. In the Meserete Kristos Church experience of non-formal theological education in Ethiopia we see an outstanding *example of organization and systematic structures as well as good programs* that facilitate not only education but also growth and spiritual maturity as well as a missionary vision of the church. We should learn from that example in my church in Spain, in Europe, and in other continents.

Another lesson is about the *concept of the believers church*. In most of our countries and especially in Spain, we have been influenced by the Catholic tradition. Even when we do not want to accept it, we have a very clerical understanding of the ministry. That means that most of the time the pastor is a professional who assumes most of the tasks. The Sunday worship services are the main religious activity when most of the members function only as a passive audience. The main feature of that meeting is the preaching that often does not have very much influence on the lives of the people. At least we do not see such a degree of consecration.

The new persons who come (if they come, since most of the Mennonite churches in Europe are growing mostly by family reproduction), those new converts soon accept the general understanding of what it means to be a member of the church and become passive spectators who see Christian life as a social status. There is a lack of teaching to prepare for action and there are no models or examples of how to do evangelism, which is almost non-existent. Internal problems and tensions among the members of the congregations grow without solutions. Applying to Europe what Bedru Hussein says, I must state that Mennonite churches in Europe are mostly impotent, bureaucratic, institutionally fossilized, and static. There may be a few exceptions.

Probably the secret is in the third lesson we have to learn from the MKC. In Europe *there is a need of renewal in the Holy Spirit*. Those Mennonite churches who have experienced such renewal have, in small scale, the same characteristics of the Ethiopian experience: people are saved, new groups are started, Christians grow to maturity, and they evangelize and disciple others. Churches grow in effectiveness answering the needs around them and they have a missionary vision. They send people to reach other groups and other cultures. This is the case of a Mennonite church in London, England, another in Longwy, northern France, and also in Spain as far as I know.

Sometimes I wonder if something should happen so that the vision of the churches in countries like Ethiopia will be brought to churches in Europe and elsewhere sending prophets from those churches where there is life and sending the pastors of those dead churches to be renewed there where the Spirit of God is in action. Some of that may be already happening.

Questions this presentation does not address in my experience as theological educator.

In Spain we are in between the rest of Europe and Africa. Our experience has the advantages and disadvantages of both continents. Spain, like other countries in Europe, is very materialistic, and more and more secularized. Pleasure and money are the goals of most of the people, even in the church. Society is continually more sophisticated and morally liberal. Abortion, divorce, good wages, the security of a good job—or a job at all, even if it is not so good—child abuse, the problems of youth, relationships in marriage,

Non-formal Theological Education

mediation in political and social conflicts are some of the current issues we have to deal with in our European context.

Probably those are also the same kinds of problems that our Ethiopian brothers and sisters have to face; or maybe they are in an entirely different world. I don't really know.

Alcoholism and drug addiction are destroying lives in Spain. AIDS is producing suffering, widows, orphans. Delinquency is forcing the building of new and bigger prisons. Immigrants, racism, rejection of the poor—we need a ministry of compassion toward those who are the outcasts of the land where we live.

In Burgos, Spain, where I come from, we have different ways of training the young believers of a twenty-year old congregation. We have our own non-formal theological school, with learning groups that are presently studying the Gospel of Matthew through materials from the South American organization SEAN—Seminary by Extension to All Nations—originally prepared in Chile. We have also used material from the evangelical charismatic renewal in Argentina called "Puerta, Camino y Meta" (The Door, the Way and the Goal). There are weekly meetings of continuing education to prepare every member of the congregation for leadership tasks in different ministries. There are discipleship classes. Dennis Byler, another of the teachers, and I are also called to do the same, during weekends in other churches elsewhere.

Probably because people do not want to risk losing their jobs, some Bible schools like the European Mennonite Bible School of Bienenberg in Switzerland have a shortage of students. There, the French section had to be closed and the German one is suffering for one or more of three reasons—lack of time, lack of money, or lack of interest.

Summer courses are also popular in some churches and there are week-long seminars during vacation time. Often, teachers from Bible schools are called to the congregations for special and intensive courses.

The fact that in Spain it is now legal to provide evangelical religious teaching in public schools has made possible the creation of schools of training mostly by extension, where people study some manuals and do the written work at home in different places and then meet once every two months for a special seminary or for exams. Most of those students are women active in Sunday schools in their congregations.

Another way of non-formal education among us has been Bible studies in home cell groups, some for new converts, others for mature Christians. The aim mostly is to help people in their practical problems and ethical questions and to prepare them for leaderships in different ministries such as children, youth, prisons and rehabilitation programs, assistance to sick persons and pastoral tasks in the different home cell groups.

Conclusion

We have a lot to learn from the MKC on church planting and lay mobilization. Our context is different and many of the problems we have to face are not part of their experience. I suppose, even when it is not stated, that the ministry of compassion and service to the poor and downcast is also among them as part of their practice and their teachings.

But the ministry of compassion for the poor and those who suffer is lacking in many Mennonite churches in Europe and North America, maybe because they think that social concern is not part of the gospel. But our experience in Burgos is that through that concern one is not only obedient to the example and teachings of Jesus but also preparing many lives to be open to receive the Lord. And we have noticed working among delinquents, those to whom much has been forgiven, give themselves fully to serve others and are the best disciples ready to learn and the best teachers ready to share with others what they have received.

Possibly one of our main tasks as educators is to prepare materials to be used in local congregations for the non-formal training of their leaders on site, without taking them away from their normal lives and practical tasks in their church and society. A few will need a more formal education. Theological schools and seminaries should more and more learn to serve the members of the congregations where they are, because cutting them from their roots brings great disorder and creates false ambitions.

I know that this is happening to many South Americans who go to seminaries in North America to be trained to serve their local churches but end up seduced by a capitalistic society of material comfort and never go back to where they came from. Thus they unjustly contribute to making the poor congregations poorer and the rich, richer. And that should also be taught in our theological schools.

RESPONSE
John Powell (USA)

"The harvest is plentiful, but the workers are few. Ask the lord of the harvest, therefore, to send out workers into his harvest field"
Luke 10:2

I am grateful to Bedru Hussein for his presentation. There are numerous issues and solutions in his presentation which help me focus on my mission in providing ministerial education in non-formal settings. Most helpful to me is his emphasis on evangelism, church planting, and structures for delivering non-formal theological education. His presentation helps refocus, for me, the hope that a theologically well prepared people can bring to an oppressive society. It also provides a framework for building a systematic approach for preparing persons for ministry.

As I view Brother Hussein's presentation, it focuses on church growth in his context. It not only focuses on growing healthy Christians, but also healthy congregations. Within that context, the focus on discipleship and discipling for healthy church renewal is very helpful. His account of the Meserete Kristos Church's focused and planned response to the spiritual needs of the people through evangelism and preparation for ministry, provides hope for church renewal. Further, the focus on the churches' response to developing leadership using the cell church model is also extremely helpful.

Throughout the ages, the church has been most successful in evangelism when it was oppressed. It is out of this context that the early church, through cells, developed. When the church became "accepted" by secular powers, it lost its focus and power. When people had lost hope because of oppression, Christians who knew God had an answer to the oppression through the anointing of the Spirit. They entered into the lives of the lost. They gave hope and the church grew because, not only did Christians "out-die" the pagan culture; they also "out-lived" and "out-thought" the pagan culture. They trained everyone to be missionaries of justice and truth.

The Meserete Kristos Church demonstrates this concept of the New Testament church—preparing persons to minister in times of chaos. Through the oppression, we see leadership and structures emerging through planned and managed educational pursuits—in cell groups and centers.

The church's four-pronged training approach is significant in providing the needed educational foci to address the needs of its members. Its emphasis on developing lay leadership is significant since it is the laity who will "grow" the church. Its focus on training the trainer and developing contextualized materials are also very helpful. A purpose for non-formal education is to mobilize the laity for church planting and evangelism. This is very important in the development of any educational program which will meet the needs of the church.

Questions and Issues

There are several questions and issues for further clarification that Brother Hussein's presentation poses for me. Let me frame some issues that need to be examined or clarified in developing non-formal theological education.

First, the experience of the Meserete Kristos Church heavily emphasizes contextualization. There seems to be an intentional emphasis focused on missiological and structural contextualization. It seems to address concerns for renewal and reform as it works toward issues of human development. It is focused also on providing the necessary structures appropriate for meeting the missiological context. Questions which need response include: How are theological and pedagogical contextualization addressed? I refer to *theological contextualization* as the educational process relating the gospel directly to urgent issues of ministry and service in the world. Does the church move itself out of its own milieu of expression of the gospel? How does it live with the tensions of competing religious expressions?

Pedagogical contextualization means dealing with issues of elitism and authoritarianism. How does non-formal theological education prepare people to overcome the dangers inherent in these issues in methods and goals so that the church can release people to servant ministry? This question must be addressed if one is designing an educational program, whether formal or non-formal, to meet the specific needs of the people.

Brother Hussein is very helpful in focusing attention on ways of structuring programs so that they can meet the needs of a region. In that regard he deals, in part, with issues relating to ministry in an urban context. In Ethiopia, tensions may develop between tribal/ethnic groups and cultures. Non-formal theological education must also address specific issues in the urban context where racial diversity presents significant tensions. "Immigrants" and people of "poor" status, based on racial and ethnic division, particularly in North American and European contexts, provide a challenge to the church. The challenge is also a barrier in preparing persons for ministry through non-formal means. A role of non-formal theological education must be to prepare persons for commitment to and working in multi-cultural and multi-racial settings.

Non-formal theological education must prepare different people to do different things. This is certainly implicit in Bedru Hussein's presentation. Within the context of preparation, we both affirm that persons must be prepared to have an understanding of the context and the nature of God in that context.

Another concern for non-formal theological education to address is "vision casting." In this instance, I believe that one of the single most important issues is *identifying and empowering visionary leaders*. I also believe that there is a need to prepare people to articulate the gospel in a classless, raceless, and genderless society. This is a role of the visionary leader. In that regard, how do we identify leaders who carry the vision? Brother Hussein tackles this question is some ways when he talks about focusing on "training trainers." To prepare visionary leaders for the harvest, non-formal theological education needs to address the challenges of identifying visionary leaders. A primary question is, Who do we train? What criteria do we use for selecting who to train? There are some choices which we need to include in addressing this issue. They are: a) Do we intentionally target more leaders than needed in our evangelism efforts?, b) Do we take risks with new people with leadership potential rather than "playing it safe" by choosing those with seniority or from the "inner circle"?, c) Do we make personal investment in a few catalytic leaders?, d) Do we advocate for our best leaders to be called and placed in greater positions of responsibility, even if they are lost to our organization and evangelistic movement? These choices will have tremendous bearing on how we structure our educational process and invest time and resources.

Another question/issue Brother Hussein's presentation raises for me is, What is the role of non-formal theological education in *helping visionary leaders form an intentional and devout prayer life?* Often we enter into problem solving and decision making without having full knowledge of what God is intending for us. In that regard, we seek to find answers through methodology and systems. In doing so, we neglect to seek the "Mind of God." This "Mind of God" is found through a devout and practicing prayer life which seeks to understand fully the nature of God. Our leaders need to be resourced in the formation of an intentional and devout prayer life which nurtures and helps clarify vision.

Another factor in the design of non-formal theological education is *ministry identity*. By ministry identity, I mean the process of exploring one's sense of call to ministry and receiving counsel on that call. Through this process, a greater self understanding of one's role in ministry may emerge. We must help people cultivate a commitment to lifelong learning about their mission in ministry. This can be done in a variety of settings which can include mentoring, small groups, lectures, discussions, course work, and practical experience. I'm calling for non-formal theological education to *focus on issues of character formation for leaders*. This should include such areas as a strong devotional life and instruction on prayer and spiritual renewal for ourselves and others in the context of our ministry, particularly in the city.

What I have discussed can be done in the context of the cell church model or traditional church structure models. I am an educator/missioner preparing people to do ministry within the urban context in the United States. In this context, the educational thrust may differ in some degree from that proposed in Brother Hussein's presentation. The Pastoral and Church Ministries Program (PCMP), which I direct in Buffalo, New York, is a program which integrates theological and practical skills for individuals who are in ministry and/or seeking to enhance their skills in "grass roots" ministry. In the PCMP we attempt to address ministry educational needs for individuals at various levels of education. These individuals participate as equals in their classroom settings and work as partners in ministry preparation. Through partnering, they develop relationships which help them focus on their particular ministry and look at their environment in different ways.

Delivery and Structure

I have attempted to raise some questions for clarification which may broaden the focus for non-formal theological education. I will briefly address some issues of delivery and structure for that education. There are numerous ways in which we can deliver theological education. Brother Hussein has discussed the concept of church-planting or regional centers, where individuals come to receive training. There are two other areas which I would like to highlight.

First, our program includes a *mentoring/coaching system* where individuals are adequately prepared in their own environment field to minister effectively before they are placed in full-time responsibility. This method requires identifying specific gifts of individuals and developing them. Those gifts may be preaching, church planting, Christian education, counseling, youth ministry, drug rehabilitation, or family and health care related ministries. In this system, one or more individuals are assigned to a "mentor/coach" who is well experienced. The mentor meets with them periodically to help focus their ministry and education. Assignments are given and individuals are assisted in developing and implementing an educational plan. Mentoring is continued until the person has reached his/her educational goal. This means that mentoring and close monitoring/assessment of leaders' skills development are individually designed and carefully planned.

A second delivery system is based on an Anabaptist/Mennonite concept of *voluntary service*. It is structured so that individuals come together and live in a community. Through a variety of educational pursuits, they learn and experience ministry together for a period of time. This training may be for 6-12 months or longer. This structure may be primarily a Western concept; however, some form of this might be implemented in any culture.

Another area that needs attention is the continuous evaluation of the program. This is important as non-formal programs seek to be continually relevant to their communities and students. Changing realities in the community demand that we continually update program foci. This means that we need to be constantly seeking creative delivery systems. The curricula must be periodically evaluated to assure that the needs of persons at various levels of education and individual ministry foci are met.

Conclusion

These are but a few of my thoughts as I respond to Brother Hussein's presentation. I offer my reflections to you for consideration and discussion. The need for workers in the harvest is great. The harvest is God's and we must respond proactively, boldly and creatively. We must remember that our communities are in spiritual chaos. New strategies and leadership skills are demanded which call for renewed leadership and vision. We need to evaluate how we do ministry. We need to evaluate how we educate our people to continually minister effectively. Not everyone can receive formal theological education; however, we can prepare people to effectively minister and bring people into the kingdom of God through a variety of non-formal educational methodologies.

As Luke 10:2 emphasizes, "The harvest is plentiful, but the workers are few". The church must pray that God will send workers for the harvest. The church must also pray for the provision of education so that the workers can meet the challenges which will face them in the field of harvest. The Christian church must be diligent in raising up well informed, highly skilled and spiritually alive leaders for our churches. God has given the vision to us; now we must respond by providing the necessary resources and skills for the harvest. I hope that my input will help toward that end.

RESPONSE
Helen Dueck (Canada/Bolivia)

Initial Reaction to Meserete Kristos Church Experience

Upon my first reading of the report by our brother Bedru I felt like saying "Wow! Could that happen in Bolivia today, or for that matter, in any other place?" My faith in the unexplainable power of the Holy Spirit tells me: "Yes, all things are possible to those who believe, to those who are called according to God's purpose!" Praise God for the wonders God is working in Ethiopia.

Then I stopped to wonder: What has happened at other times in history when there has been phenomenal growth? When traveling through the Near East we looked for signs of the New Testament church in Corinth and Thessalonica. We wondered what had happened to the strong Mennonite churches in Europe, the cradle of Anabaptism; or in the Methodist or Baptist churches of Bolivia after the rapid expansion at the turn of this century; or in Uruguay after the sixties? Has the church not been faithful in its outreach? In its education programs? Do we need more persecution? Are the educational programs not effective?

The Evangelical Mennonite Church of Bolivia

The Mennonite Church in Bolivia was born as a direct outgrowth of MCC presence. In 1960 MCC responded to the needs of a group of Mennonite settlers of European background. Soon the administrators and volunteers became aware of the tremendous need for development aid to the Bolivian peasants. (In 1988 the rural literacy rate was 68%, life expectancy 49.5 years, and per capita income $US700.) Through sacrificial toil and lifestyle models the volunteers shared their faith and people came to know the Lord. MCC asked the Mennonite mission agencies to send workers to help the four fledgling churches.

Where the church is born through development work, and literacy classes, the profile of the first generation Christians is different than where "church planting" is a programmed mission. In Bolivia the believers were concerned and caring but did not have the academic tools to organize or structure their programs of ministry. Furthermore, the mission agencies had just learned in other countries that withdrawal of financial support for national workers and programs was very painful and they did not want to repeat the experience in Bolivia. The churches were too poor to support "pastors" so they were encouraged to develop lay leadership teams. My husband and I have stood in amazement at the wisdom of the leaders, at the simple trust in the midst of socioeconomic adversity and the desire to be a witnessing community.

The MKC Model

Pastoral Care Structure. I begin with the third of the changes listed in the Background section. The MKC model is helpful in its emphasis on groups that meet for prayer, Bible study, mutual concern and fellowship. I'm not sure that the "structure" of the local church outlined would be effective in our small Bolivian churches. The "training committee" would work better at the *junta* (conference) level with representation from each of the five churches. The reports of the local churches are heard at the monthly meetings of the *junta* and the annual assembly elects officers and discusses program needs. It would be very helpful to strengthen local cell groups and see to it that the groups of new converts get to the next stage of training.

The Bolivian church has struggled with "imported" study guides. One hopes and dreams of the time when the local conference would be able to prepare its own materials.

Training Program for Selected Trainers. I don't really understand what "structured non-formal training" means. Would that include preparation for personal evangelism? From the document it would appear that the thrust is on deepening the spiritual experience of the selected trainers. It is noteworthy that you look for themes that are relevant to the needs of the churches. Several questions arise: Where do the trainees receive the Bible knowledge and teaching experience listed in the criteria for the educational system? Am I right to assume that the emphasis on the curriculum lies on expansion?

One Year for Christ Non-formal Training Program. Some of the processes to recruit, equip and send young people would be useful. The training, evaluation and experience could enhance the program that the Bolivian church together with MCC is engaged in. Several questions:
1. Are no women given this opportunity?
2. Does the program include any holistic or community ministry such as health, education, agriculture?

3. What teaching methods are employed: lecture, discussion, investigation and discovery, other?

Curriculum. There appears to be considerable emphasis on doctrine and practical theology (100 hours) over against 60 hours of Bible and 30 hours of hermeneutics. Does the MKC doctrine include any Anabaptist history and theology? Do the students come with a knowledge of the Bible story, an encounter with the God who has manifested Godself in the history of God's chosen people?

Other Concerns

Non-formal Education. There are different definitions of non-formal education. Some refer to the learning that takes place when the church worships and celebrates together. Others think of the teaching/learning described in Deuteronomy 6 and the learning through positive (or negative) relationships and experiences. The Fifth Annual Institute for Studies in Non-formal Education, Michigan State University, 1983, says: "Non-formal education is not just a theoretical category of the social processes of learning.... In most cases it is concerned with the human learning tasks associated with a particular program of social change."

The same institute describes learnings as *participatory* and *anticipatory*. Perhaps Paulo Freire embodies these terms when he speaks of *conscientization*; providing experiences whereby the participants reflect on their situation and then become involved in the needed changes.

It would seem that for our purpose we would understand the term non-formal as providing learning experiences that would aid the church in its change or growth: spiritual, numerical, lifestyle, and witness in word and deed.

Models of Non-formal Teaching/Learning.
1. The committee had chosen evangelism as one of the topics for study at a leaders retreat. The thirty-plus participants were divided into groups of four. They were given a biblical text and questions: who was the evangelist, who the person/s, what method was used (conversation, sermon, encounter, etc.) and what was the result. The groups eagerly examined the text and brought their findings to the plenary session where they were charted on large sheets of paper. A lively discussion on different methods of evangelism followed. I would call that "participatory."

2. The theme of an annual assembly was peacemaking. After an opening Bible study different groups prepared skits to show what might happen if they applied these biblical principles to their real life situations. "Anticipatory," don't you think?

3. Josefina, a dear peasant woman whose only academic training was learning to read with the help of MCC volunteers, wanted to do more than teach the village girls to knit. She told me: "I told them the story of the ten virgins. Do you think that was all right?" This was an example of the oldest non-formal education, storytelling.

In Summary

Brother Bedru has presented us with an example of a rapidly growing community of believers in Ethiopia. He has suggested that the organization is constantly being evaluated and restructured to meet new challenges. The educational programs, both formal and non-formal, involve the congregations as teachers/learners. This seems to address the situation of a large, strong national Christian movement.

There are, however, smaller, younger, groups that struggle to be the church; to grow according to their limited resources. God is blessing the efforts of faithful followers, perhaps not as easily measured or counted but according to their faith and faithfulness.

4

Formal Theological Education: The Centre and the Boundaries

Lydia Neufeld Harder (Canada)

Creative leadership is often done in the space between *vision* and *current reality*, between seeing clearly where we want to be and telling the truth of where we actually are. The energy which can move an institution toward a new vision comes when both a compelling picture of the future is accepted and an accurate picture of current reality is given.[1] Daniel Schipani has given us a vision that is inspiring and thought-provoking in its scope and depth— "theological education for the sake of the church in the world in the light of God's reign". In a much less comprehensive way, I want to describe my own context of work as part of the reality which must be put into juxtaposition with Daniel's vision. The tensions that are generated when I place vision and reality side by side create the challenges I face in my role, whether as board member, as administrator, or as teacher. I will therefore speak concretely, referring directly to the two institutions to which I relate— Associated Mennonite Biblical Seminary and Toronto Mennonite Theological Centre. I hope that you will respond by also describing your own realities and your own challenges.

THE CENTRE AND THE BOUNDARY

I want to begin by using spatial imagery to describe my context. This imagery is suitable because formal educational institutions are often identified with buildings and campuses which have an inside and an outside separated by a wall or other visible boundary marker. Moreover, this imagery has been used in discussions of theological education by a number of different writers. I will draw on two sources in order to reflect both critically

---

[1] Eugene Hansell, "The Seminary as a Learning Organization: A Systems Approach", unpublished paper presented to Board of Trustees and Faculty of Associated Mennonite Biblical Seminaries (June 3, 1993), p.3.

and creatively on the centre and the boundaries of formal educational institutions.

The first source, Walter Brueggeman, uses the imagery of a wall to talk about two kinds of theological conversation that need to take place in a church context.[2] The first conversation takes place "behind the wall" and uses communal language to speak to the insiders of the faith community and to God. In this conversation reality is defined by the faith and conviction that God is alive and active in the world. The second conversation takes place "on the wall" in a "foreign" tongue. This more public conversation uses language which assumes a different view of the world and is constructed around the dominant perceptions of reality by the larger society. In this conversation the contributions of the faith community are often marginal and controversial.

In Brueggeman's way of using this imagery the boundary or wall refers to the place where the differing perspectives of the faith community and the society surrounding it meet. Sometimes this meeting is friendly, creating new insights for both. Sometimes this meeting is confrontational or even hostile. Choices must then be made by both the society and the theological community about the world-view that will guide its life and work. The choices that the church makes in this public arena reflect on the integrity of the language used behind the wall.

In a quite different way, a number of liberation theologians also speaks about the "centre" and the "margins". However, in their use of these terms these theologians are referring to differing social/political locations as defined by sociology and political science.[3] This imagery arises out of the insight that our social context, whether within or outside of a particular church setting, influences our theology. Here the centre refers to the dominant group in the scholarly or church community that determines the agenda addressed in theology. The marginal refers to those with

---

[2] "The Legitimacy of a Sectarian Hermeneutic," *Interpretation and Obedience: From Faithful Reading to Faithful Living*, (Minneapolis: Fortress Press, 1991), pp. 41-69.

[3] An example: Christopher Rowland, "In this Place: The Centre and the Margins in Theology", Fernando F. Segovia and Mary Ann Tolbert, eds., *Reading From This Place: Social Location and Biblical Interpretation in Global Perspective*, Vol. 2 (Minneapolis: Fortress Press, 1995), pp. 169-182.

fewer resources who are confined to the edge of the community. Their voice is often silenced because no one is listening to them. In liberation theology's use of this imagery, those who stand on the wall are not there by choice but rather are pushed into that place by those in the centre of the community.

Christian educational institutions can be described using both of these frameworks because these institutions not only represent the church but also are concrete social/political entities in themselves. The questions that I will raise have to do with issues of power and authority, the agenda raised by liberation theology. However, the definition of power and authority is more ambiguous and fluid than liberation theology would admit. This is so because definitions may vary depending on where you stand in relationship to the wall as defined by Brueggeman. The ambiguity will become visible as we move from self-evident definitions to a more complex analysis of the challenges facing these institutions.

A Preliminary Description

At first glance it is easy to name Associated Mennonite Bible Seminary (AMBS) as a school located at the centre of the faith community. As an inter-Mennonite educational institution committed to the Anabaptist heritage it is crucially located in the *centre* of North American Mennonite church life. It has as its purpose the "preparing of pastors, missionaries, teachers, evangelists, and other church leaders," that is, persons called to be at the centre of church life. The resources of its community include buildings, books, professors, administrators, and a heritage of education for the Mennonite church that goes back more than 100 years.

In contrast, Toronto Mennonite Theological Centre (TMTC), an inter-Mennonite teaching and resource centre at the Toronto School of Theology, can rather quickly be understood as standing on the boundaries of the church community. Its purpose—to "foster reflection on the Anabaptist-Mennonite heritage by graduate students (doctoral level) and scholars in theology within an ecumenical context"—suggests conversation that goes beyond the Mennonite community. Its location on the largest university campus in Canada implies that its language will be public, dominated by the rational criteria of the university. Its immediate resources are limited, with a budget under $30,000, two part-time faculty, 15-20 students who relate to the centre in an informal way, and a history of less than ten years. It owns no building but instead uses the resources of its host, the Toronto School of Theology. Its constituency, the North American Mennonite church, is largely unaware of its existence, though it represents the only Mennonite institution in North America devoted to doctoral-level work.

In my role as a board member for AMBS and as the director and a teacher at TMTC I have reflected on the significance of boundaries and walls for the identity and work of these two institutions. I have discovered that some of the central issues that have arisen for me in my work have to do with the meaning attached to the walls and boundaries that our institutional communities represent for the larger church community and for the society around us. I have realized that the above characterization of the two schools is inaccurate, largely because margins and walls, inside and centre mean something different depending on where you are standing when you speak.

As I become immersed in the practical decisions that I need to make I realize that formal educational institutions reflect how we understand the church in the world. The choices and commitments that I make in my work affect the way the boundaries are fixed not only of the educational institution but also of the church. Therefore a closer look must be taken to see how the centre is determined and what the boundaries of the community represent to the various members of the church and society.

CHOICES AND COMMITMENTS

The choices that each church institution needs to make have to do with its identity. This identity can be described in terms of Schipani's description of the church's three-fold reason for being. I will therefore frame the discussion of boundaries by asking three key questions which these institutions must answer in relationship to the church's worship, community, and mission:

Which language do we use? (The question of *worship*)
Brueggeman has suggested that Christians need to be bilingual.[4] They must be conversant in the language of the faith

---

[4]Brueggeman p. 43.

Formal Theological Education

community where they speak in their own "sectarian" language in order to discuss issues of identity and commitment to God. However, Christians who are faithful to a sense of mission in the world, must also be ready to enter the public dialogue where they must speak in a foreign tongue, enter into discussion of agenda that goes beyond their own community, and encounter differing and often conflicting perceptions of reality.

Mennonites who have a history of being a minority religion and a separated people have a long tradition of what can be called sectarian conversation. This has allowed them to concentrate on being the church rather than accommodating themselves to the dominant culture of the day. There is, however, a temptation associated with this conversation. Sometimes "church" language has become exclusive refusing access to those from the outside who would wish to enter our faith communities. Some people who do not fit the image of a Mennonite church member have been silenced or given no authority to address the community.

More recently another subtle temptation has entered our communities. As we have gained respectability in our society we have begun to seek academic recognition by entering the public conversation. This conversation has put us in dialogue with other theological institutions that have arisen in the larger context of Christendom, a context in which the interpretation of reality by society at large has sometimes been assumed to be Christian. Therefore the relationship between church and society has tended to be friendly, with only minor tensions arising between theological institutions and the university. The language commonly used in formal theology has more and more become the language of the reigning rationality of the day, whether that be philosophy, psychology, history, or sociology. The temptation for theology then has been to mistake the foreign language for its own mother tongue, thus allowing the public language to determine its interpretation of reality.

Mennonite students often feel that they are presented with a choice that does not allow them to become truly bilingual. Either they can stay with the biblical language of the community and risk withdrawal into a private sphere of social reality which has nothing to say to the broader world or they can use the foreign language of society and risk being seduced by the dominant rationality of the established culture.

This dilemma faces us at TMTC in a particular way because we are part of the larger university complex as well as part of an ecumenical institution which has fostered particularly friendly relationships to the university. I well remember being faced with the choice of disciplines as I entered doctoral work. I could enter the biblical department where historical norms were dominant and where I would be discouraged from wrestling with contemporary meanings of the Bible, or I could enter the systematic theology department where the Bible was seldom referred to and philosophical considerations were primary. It seemed impossible to study the Bible as a real source for contemporary theology related to congregational life. As a teacher I continue to wrestle with this issue as I design courses and advise students in the context of a theological school whose existence depends on a friendly relationship with the university.

AMBS is also faced with the choice of language. However, because AMBS is a Mennonite seminary with a primary dependence on the congregations for its existence, its temptation may be somewhat different. Students and professors can easily assume that the language of the Mennonite community and its view of reality can be fully equated with divine revelation. They can then fail to notice when their separate existence becomes exclusive and oppressive; they can ignore the prophetic voices on the margin of the community. At the same time it is often difficult to notice the subtle influence of the values of the society around us which have become disguised in community talk. This creates a situation in which our theology has no unique resources to assist those living and working in the public arena.

The question of language is a question of primary loyalty and authority; therefore it is an issue of worship. Choosing a language means choosing a view of reality which will determine both the conversation behind the wall and the conversation on the wall. This view of reality must always be based on the reign of God in both the church and in the world. Learning to worship in order to be open to God's revealing and transforming presence is the antidote to the temptations of idolatry that can be found both in the centre and on the margins of the faith community. Only worship can help us maintain our identity without creating false boundaries. Both AMBS and TMTC are struggling to know how to do this with integrity.

Formal Theological Education

Which resources do we draw on? (The question of *community*)

In asking the question of resources our minds very quickly move to two kinds of resources that are valued by the educational community, the resource of finances and the resource of leadership personnel. In fact at AMBS we have used the term "partnership" to describe the relationship between the congregation and the institution. In this partnership the congregations provide the necessary funds to gain a secure financial base for the school while the school provides the training for the churches' leaders.

However, it is exactly in this simply stated relationship that many of the issues related to community lie. This is so because power and authority are often dependent on who controls the finances and who chooses the leaders. Thus it is easy for persons within educational institutions to begin to vie for power and to compete for status. In this struggle the persons on the margins are sometimes forgotten and competition between people and between institutions begins to happen. Several issues could be named:

a) Who defines what good leadership looks like? Is it the congregations? If so, the training of leaders should take place in the context of a congregation rather than on a campus isolated from the issues of the church. Or should it be the knowledge learned from scholarly study whether this is from biblical studies or from psychology or sociology? Then leadership training should have a more scholarly disciplined focus on academic courses. Who decides this question? Is it the professors, the congregational members, the students, or the board who all have vested interest in the answer to this question? How do we bring all of these people into the conversation while focusing on a vision that goes beyond each person's personal interest?

b) Who decides which institution should receive the most funds? Is it the conference or the congregations or the individuals who have the most funds to give? It is becoming more evident how difficult it is for institutions to co-operate and how difficult it is to fund all of them. Some institutions will not survive the financial cutbacks that are now taking place. Which ones should survive?

c) Who should receive financial assistance for their theological education? Should it be the brightest of our young people? Or the ones coming from our white middle-class congregations? Or the male members of the community? Or should our resources instead be used to fund education for members of our minority groups who are unable to fund their own education?

Both AMBS, an established seminary, and TMTC, a new institution, are struggling with the relationship between finances and leadership. But perhaps what is needed is to look again at how we define what is included in the notion of a resource. We might discover that our educational communities need the handicapped, those of non-white races, women and men of all ages and of a variety of social backgrounds. We would welcome the participation of those from other countries, from other denominations and from other races. Decisions might be easier to make if we would look at how we could co-operate together to make our educational communities reflect the rich diversity of the body of Christ.

Whose agenda receives attention? (The question of *mission*)

Daniel Schipani has diagrammed the various agendas that interrelate in diverse ways in theological education. He has suggested that there may be a certain tension which arises as these agendas intersect. He has placed the dimension of human emergence, both personal and social, in the centre of the agenda for theological education. What he has not been able to do is diagram the complex nature of this emergence in light of God's reign.

As the church becomes involved in mission it becomes involved in situations of sin and evil. Victims of oppression and domination, persons bound by habits and customs which do not reflect God's reign, cry out for liberation and healing. But rational education alone does not heal. Nor do ecclesial communities long embroiled in conflict and dissension learn shalom by only talking about it. A society that has become insensitive to the poor needs more than prophetic preaching to change. How do theological institutions foster both formation of character and transformation of persons and communities?

One practical question that arises for educators who take mission seriously is the question of requirements and evaluation of students' work. Transformation is difficult to measure and standard tests do not fit each person. AMBS has struggled with finding ways to be more closely involved with each person in the process of completing an MDiv. Integration papers are discussed with peers. Self evaluations are required throughout the process. But the task of fostering real change continues to be the biggest challenge.

What is needed is finding ways to invite God's transforming Spirit into the midst of the learning community. Perhaps this invitation comes most powerfully through the witness of the Bible and the testimony of changed people and communities. Thus any theological institution must be vitally connected to the centre of its curriculum—the Bible, and to persons and communities that exhibit transformation by the grace of God. Careful discernment is needed to invite this witness into the classrooms and to take the students out into the world to recognize God's work in the world.

At TMTC I have been given the task of finding ways of enriching the curriculum of students studying at the doctoral level by arranging forums and inviting speakers. Many of my daily decisions have to do with building connections between life outside of the library and the theory written in books. Sometimes this connection is made through a new look at our own history in the Anabaptist reformation. At other times it is made by inviting in someone from the ecumenical or global community to speak to us. Our most intense meetings often have to do with the question of our personal relationship to the Bible. The temptation is to stay with safe topics that do not question the status quo and to focus on academic issues divorced from personal commitment. But it is exactly in the personal interactions that students are faced most directly with their need for divine empowering.

AMBS is rich with resources that witness to God's power. What does this mean for the city in which the seminary is located? What does this mean for persons seeking healing within the community? The connections between daily life on campus and the task of empowering for mission are often difficult to find. AMBS has tried to struggle with this by its focus on practical pastoral education and the opportunities that are given for community involvement. However, both receiving God's healing and sharing God's invitation do not come easily to persons comfortable in their own pew in church.

IN THE LIGHT OF GOD'S REIGN

Though AMBS and TMTC are very different institutions they share in common their primary context—the reign of God in the world—and a common task—formal theological education. In their vocation of enabling for worship, equipping for community and empowering for mission they struggle with focusing on the centre as they break down barriers and invite persons beyond their boundaries to come and learn of God's grace. To do this they must become bilingual, they must learn to recognize and share available resources and they must be able to invite vital witnesses to God's transformation into their midst.

Our analysis has hinted that both institutions will not naturally move in the direction of God's reign. Temptations which deny God and God's way of being in the world are there for persons involved in both institutions. In that sense both institutions must affirm again and again their dependence on the larger church's discernment and counsel. They must be ready to change, to live and even to die in the service of God in the world.

As educators we have been given the task to give creative leadership to the churches' task of theological reflection. May God help us to see a clear vision of where the church is to be and to tell the truth about the institutions in which we work.

RESPONSE

Bruce Khumalo (Zimbabwe)

E.W. Blyden (1832-1912), a West Indian of Ibo (African) descent, was an educational philosopher during the colonial period. He addressed the issues of making black Africa a respected and important participant in the world community, how to improve conditions for Africans, and how to dispel the myth of the inferiority of black people. The main solution for him was through the reform of the educational system. Reform of the educational system is important since education as we have it originally came from the West and was meant to prolong colonial rule and the subjugation of other races.

If education is to serve a liberating purpose it has to change. Through formal education people can rise from a background of insignificance to that of empowerment and ability to participate in development. Education's real goal is the self-actualization of those involved. But missionary education was not as such. The fundamental goal of education is to develop people for their own sake, not to convert them. Education is a basic human right. Schools are places where one ought to experience new values, new ideas, new opinions, and new concepts, a place where one's whole outlook on life is changed. Schools are vehicles of transformation. It is also the right of everyone to hear about God, and the duty of the church to reach out and make disciples, but this is a different task from that of education.

Formal education as a melting pot

Ideas are brewed there as both the tutor and student body interact. Worldviews are as many as the number of people in the classroom. A great deal of money is spent on buildings and learning aids. Whether the students learn or not, the money is spent under the assumption that learning will take place. However, this is not always the case. The dream and concepts of formal education are western. The African ideology of education is based on apprenticeship, that is, applied, hands-on exercise. *Learning in the African context is learning for life.* This is to enable the learner to be relevant in his or her setting. In Zimbabwe there are a lot of school leavers who are misfits in society and very irrelevant. Their formal education, whether high school, college, university, or seminary, gave them wrong assumptions. These former students might have educational documents but are unable to deliver the goods. It has been my concern that we do not have enough African theologians in our Anabaptist family of churches. We quickly begin to think of theologians coming from Europe and North America to teach. These teachers, however, work with concepts in their own mother tongues. No wonder we are having so much trouble initiating indigenous theologians when they need to capture theological precepts in an exotic language.

In the area of theological education, the African ways of learning could lead to more relevant church rituals. For example, eating the bread and drinking the cup in communion is an empty ritual if people fail to share emotionally and economically with one another. The idea of being dead to sin represented by baptism might make more sense to Africans if the symbol used were a grave or a coffin. The way water is used in our culture leads people to understand water baptism as the way to wash away their sins.

Theological education can be either deep or shallow. A major problem leading to shallowness is that most study materials and the concepts they represent are in a foreign language. The interpretive paradigm is western. I myself, for example, after many years of teaching and studying in English, still dream in my mother tongue, Ndebele. Can TE get below the surface as long as people are learning in a foreign language? TE also needs to integrate formal and practical aspects. Students should be required to demonstrate their learning in visible ways. They should also be empowered for mission, as well as for deeper discoveries about themselves. *The pedagogical approach should be human-centered* rather than simply concept-centered. Entry qualifications themselves create problems, since they represent a society where a superiority or caste system is attached to educational background. Such standards themselves suggest education for prestige rather than for service.

Among problems we have experienced in our formal TE programs in Zimbabwe are the *pressures of the curriculum*. The teacher wants to finish the syllabus, and the student wants to pass the exam with distinction. We might work at shifting this dynamic by requiring practical courses like evangelism and church planting, which would ask students to be involved in planting a congregation before they are eligible to graduate. Practical skills which make self-support feasible, such as carpentry, sewing, and farming, should be included in the curriculum. We should encourage a respect for people who work with their hands.

Another important problem, which is also reflected in Lydia Harder's paper, is *the problem of structures and power*. We spend a great deal of time in staff meetings, and we have to meet and discuss our programs with the president of the Bible college, the bishop of the church, the general conference of the church, and the donor agencies (mission agencies). Needing to deal with all these levels of bureaucracy discourages vision because it takes energy trying to sell our vision. We are often expected to dance to the tune of those with power.

The church is a living organism, a body with many members. This living body is the dwelling place of the Holy Spirit. As we have heard, the church has a threefold reason for being: worship, or building our relationship with God; community, building our relationships to each other; and mission, extending relationships to the global society. The church and its ministries are not the same thing. The church is people, the ministries are the revelation of the church's existence as a living organism. *The purpose of our theological education needs to be both to support the ministries and extend the body.*

RESPONSE
Jaime Prieto (Costa Rica)

What I find useful in this presentation for my work

The central aspect of the presentation of Lydia Harder's input which is most helpful to me in the ministry of formal education is the confirmation that the service offered to the church by universities and seminaries in the tasks of God's reign always confronts difficulties, limitations, and new challenges from its own context. In this regard we must record the dynamic of theological education which, tied to the word, is at the same time—as Paulo Freire said—bearer of a creative, transformative action which should lead to a synthesis between action and reflection.

It is important to point out also the way in which Lydia has utilized the theoretical concepts of Walter Brueggemann and Christopher Rowland; for example the image of "barriers," and the distortions of authority and power which appear in theological education institutions. These theoretical fundamentals serve the author as model in order to confront the reality of her teaching practice.

Lydia bases her observations on her administrative experiences as a leader and an instructor in two Mennonite institutions, and from that perspective notes the differences and at the same time the mutual demands of her daily educational practice, all in reference to the vision presented in the paper by Daniel Schipani. Said in another way, she does not reject the stated vision, but rather places it alongside her daily teaching practice. And in signaling the tensions, difficulties and challenges in which she is involved at Associated Mennonite Biblical Seminary and at the Toronto Mennonite Theological Centre, she calls us also, all of us who work in the field of theological education, to think deeply about our own daily educational practice. A relevant fact in the presentation of Lydia Harder is that she both identifies herself as Mennonite and also acknowledges the limitations of denominational identity in order to open herself more broadly to what we understand as "the reign of God." From that identification, only by critical reflection is she able to underline both the benefits and the limitations of the theological centers where she is involved as a leader. We always need to be self-critical so that we do not fall into the temptation of conformity and superior power as well as the educational limitations experienced by our institutions and formal theological programs.

The tension which the author has wanted to maintain between the vision of Daniel Schipani and the reality which she confronts in her daily experience is evident as she evaluates the options and commitments of theological education in relationship to worship, community, and mission. The various questions which she raises in respect to the commitments of theological education are related to her daily practice, yet at the same time she places us outside these questions. I think that this is a good method to hold onto in any theological education program. We need to hold out new and utopian visions in these difficult times, but they must take evaluative form and new impulses growing out of our practical experiences. Only when we are willing to live in the tension between the vision and practical reality, and experience the mutual correction which comes from that tension, will we be able as a church to see and walk in transforming ways in the light and the rays of God's reign.

Questions I have as a theological educator which are not represented

As an introduction to this part of my response I would like to clarify that the observations and questions I have come from my practical involvement in the Latin American Biblical Seminary, an interdenominational institution, with a mission of theological formation for very diverse cultural contexts throughout Latin America. My first questions have to do with the theory of Brueggemann and Rowland. Brueggemann was reflecting about the barriers (walls) which language presents when it is in use, whether it may be "public" or even "foreign" in contexts outside of the university or the community life of the churches. Lydia as well as Brueggemann postulates the necessity of utilizing a bilingual form of communication which would allow the establishment of bridges between the church and the modern world, between the world and the general public and the particular life of the Mennonite communities, and finally, between the secular world and the rural world of Mennonites. What about other contexts in Anabaptist communities, where the barriers of communication have to do not only with the relationship between the language of the rational and intellectual and the daily life of the community, but also where communication barriers grow up because of diversity of cultures? Rowland also speaks of the concentration of authority and power in certain persons in educational centers where theology is done, as well as the marginalization of those in the community who are not sufficiently informed of the themes being discussed.

In Rowland's analysis, this question is presented in a very general form, without achieving a clear description of who those marginalized people are. In Latin America, we see that the word "marginalized" or "poor" is not sufficient to describe those who have no power or authority to make decisions in theological institutions. We are constantly able to speak of *mestizo*, indigenous, and black communities who find themselves marginalized from the political and theological directors of ecclesiastical centers. In this regard the ambiguity of power becomes more conflictive because it crosses racial and/or cultural questions. How do we incorporate other variant perspectives which interfere in the struggle for power and authority of theological institutions? It appears to me that the theories of Brueggemann and Rowland are essentially theoretical, and help to question the educative role of Mennonite institutions in North America, but is their analysis insufficient for the multicultural reality of Latin America? Will it be necessary, to paraphrase the words of Jean-Paul Sartre, that "the mouths open themselves," so that "the yellow and black voices reproach the inhumanity" which is present in the power struggles in the midst of our theological institutions?

In reference to theological education as in the service of training for worship, Lydia proposes as a solution to communication barriers efforts to relate the language of the public sphere with the conventional language of the faith community. Nevertheless, we recognize that the problem of communication transcends what we traditionally know as spoken or written language (words, vocabulary), since we also need to take into account the language of symbols, of gestures, of the body, which never shows itself the same way among *mestizo*, white, indigenous, and black groups. Today a whole series of rituals and symbols exist which have already lost their meaning within the community. On the other hand, an entirely new group of symbols and rituals have emerged which have renewed the different cultures of Latin America. From this reality my questions emerge:

* How will theological education contribute to making place for a polyphonic language (symbols, myths, songs, body movements, gestures, etc.) of our peoples in worship?
* How can we assist our theological education to revitalize our concepts of worship in such a way that we can perceive that in the latter days, as the prophet Joel said (2.28): "God will pour out the Spirit on all flesh," and this means nothing less than that the Spirit Itself transcends all barriers of race, culture, language, or sex, and flows freely over all persons? I myself am witness to the flow and suppleness of the Spirit of God, manifested in bodily trances, in murmurs, in new tongues, tears and sighs, both in the experience of brothers and sisters of the "Terreiros" of Candomblé in Rio de Janeiro and among charismatic Mennonite groups in Heredia, Costa Rica. How does theological education help us so that we do not allow to disappear this suppleness of God, in different faces—our faces—in order to change our heart of stone into a heart of flesh and in order to fill us with our first love (Rev. 2.4), uniting *mestizo*, white, indigenous, yellow, and black hands?

The questions about theological education and mission are born out of my experiences with persons of different religious expressions. They are not only Mennonites or persons who claim Christian faith; I refer to my encounter with sisters and brothers for whom it is not incompatible to associate their religious inheritance coming from their own cultures with Christian elements.

I also have met other sisters and brothers who want to continue to deepen their faith and spirituality which comes from a millenarian spiritual and cultural heritage, which often enters into contradiction with the form in which Christians understand revelation. Lydia Harder mentioned that the reality of oppression which is experienced in the world requires not only a rational but also a liberating education. In this same perspective, we understand that the truth grows, developing and revealing the same process of liberation (Jn 8.31-32), without negating the sociocultural memory of our peoples. Thus we ask: How can formal theological education continue to offer a space for reflection about God, pastoral formation, and reality without negating the cultural foundations of our peoples? In the Latin American Biblical Seminary, we have had some indigenous Christian students whose theses question our academic curriculum. Prudencio Quispe from Peru, for example, gives much importance in his study to the necessity of including their own courses in a curriculum, such as: a) Theological and anthropological resources in order to rediscover religions and cultures; b) Quechua spirituality and theology; c) Quechua, Pag'os and Yatiri priests.

I see as a further priority the importance of including courses within the curriculum of Andean theological training which deal with a) Quechua cosmology, and b) Quechua myths and legends; also courses in the field of mission which consider a) mission and indigenous resistance, b) cultural identity and inculturation, c) living together in unity (Chulla Kawsay) and d) building of utopia from within the church, that is Quechua community and organization.

Growing out the history of the Mennonites as an immigrant minority, Lydia has spoken of formal theological education as a bridge of communication which assists Mennonites to give witness to their faith in the modern world. In the current situation of Latin America, the following crucial questions can be posed:

* What is to be the function of theological education in order to help us to give reason for the foundation of our faith?
* How did Menno Simons, quoting the Apostle Paul (1 Cor. 3.11), say that the way of our liberation is Christ, but at the same time help us to recognize that "God is able to open other means of access" for the liberation of other men and women? (I prefer to speak of liberation before speaking of salvation because of the fullness of its connotation.)
* How can formal theological education be a communication bridge where Anabaptist faith convictions, rather than assimilating, co-opting, or changing other religious expressions of faith which are present in cultures founded in indigenous, African-American or Asian cultures, is capable to lead toward universal shalom, to serve the communion table in order to share in the midst of a polyphony of voices the profound mysteries of God?

RESPONSE
V.K. Rufus (India)

My response has three parts:

I agree and support Lydia on the following points:
 * Theological education needs to be bilingual, in the primary as well as the secondary sense that she suggests. Church members and students must be practically bilingual to communicate the gospel in Indian contexts. Theological schools should prepare students to develop this ability. I am involved in training people in our college for bilingual communication.
 * Our theological training institutions also struggle with questions of power and authority.
 * I agree with Lydia's statements on the task of theological education (TE) as quoted from Daniel Schipani's paper.
 * Lydia has described well the problem of money. Money is a central problem in our theological schools. In our setting we are trying to pay attention to this problem. We are making an effort to provide opportunities for poor students, for those from marginal communities, for women, and for those from nondenominational backgrounds.

In her discussion of the two institutions, Lydia presents different approaches to TE.
 I suggest that formal TE needs both kinds of environments in order to provide the best preparation. I agree with Lydia that the Bible as relevant to actual life situations should be central to all our TE efforts.

Concerns
 * *Anabaptist theology*. I am concerned about those lecturing in our theological training institutions in India. We do not have enough teachers who have had training in Anabaptist theology. I urge those involved in this consultation to provide opportunities for training seminars for our teachers.
 * *Resources*. I agree with Lydia that we should use available resources. We need to find approaches which benefit the students. I appeal to the institutions in rich countries and churches

for exchanges of teachers, visiting lecturers, sharing of books, and financial assistance to our TE programs.

This paper has encouraged me to continue to be involved in formal TE, despite the problems that we face.

RESPONSE
Bernhard Ott (Switzerland)
Introduction

Let me begin with a word of thanks to Daniel Schipani and Lydia Harder; Daniel for the *vision* of theological education he has presented to us, and Lydia for bringing this vision down to reality. I appreciate her introduction in which she places our reflections on theological education "in the space between *vision* and *current reality*." I can—in the light of my own experience—only affirm that this is really the space where the daily struggle for meaningful theological training takes place. My response will also focus on *vision* and *reality*. My current reality in terms of formal theological education is twofold as indicated below.

The first reality is that of the European Mennonite Bible School at Bienenberg, Switzerland, where I serve as academic dean. It is a small Bible institute founded in 1950, serving the churches in Germany, France, and Switzerland with programs in the French and the German languages. The primary task of the Bienenberg Bible Institute was not professional pastoral training, but the education of lay workers and leaders for the church through non-degree programs up to two years. Like many other Bible institutes in North America and Europe, our school faces severe problems. Changing educational needs, economic insecurities, the lifestyle of a new generation, and many other realities have caused a decrease in student enrolment. The introduction of an additional college level program, the accreditation of the school, as well as the implementation of a variety of extension programs have not yet led out of the crisis situation. This is one reality.

The second reality is represented by my personal involvement in a project to establish a theological seminary in the German-speaking context of Europe for pastoral and leadership training on the Master's level. Such a project has been discussed for many years and is now about to be realised in connection with the European Mennonite Bible School at Bienenberg. These are the realities I am experiencing. Let me now identify two areas addressed by Lydia Harder and apply them to our situation.

The issue of partnership between the educational institution and the church

Lydia Harder has pointed out the dynamics of the relationship between the churches and the educational institution in a very helpful way. I can only agree, it is occasionally a very difficult partnership, because it has to do with money and leadership. In our context I see at least two areas of tension which I will discuss briefly.

First, the theological school in its interaction with the larger ecumenical world as well as the academic world is a laboratory of free and critical reflection which often stands in tension with the maintenance-oriented forces of the denominational tradition. In this perspective, colleges and seminaries are viewed as dangerous places. And precisely these are the places where a new leadership generation is shaped, a leadership generation which most likely will implement changes in the churches—those churches which don't want to change. And all this with the money of the churches. In a certain way the churches are asked to finance the very changes which they don't desire. This puts any president, dean, or fund-raiser under severe pressure, the pressure to please the churches in order to get enough money. How do you live with this tension?

The second area has to do with leadership and decision-making. In our European Mennonite churches there is high emphasis on grass-roots democracy. Each church member, each local congregation (and in our German context even each of the small conferences) wants to be involved in the process of decision-making. There is therefore, on the one hand, the strong expectation that we as educational institution always ask the churches what they want. This expectation is based on the assumption that people at the grass-roots best know what the needs are. On the other hand there is the need for leadership. Almost all the institutions of the conferences—from mission to youth camps and from relief work to the Bible school—were not founded by conference decisions but by courageous pioneers and groups which had a vision and put it into reality. Today all these institutions are conference institutions. But how will they get a new vision for the future? In my experience, new visions are not generated in conference meetings and assemblies of delegates. The institutions of the conferences need to be unleashed to provide new vision and leadership for the church. Doing so they may come up with new and challenging ideas and then we are back to finances: Will the churches pay for educational institutions which provide disturbing and critical leadership?

The tension between academic reflection and involvement

As a third critical area Lydia Harder has identified the tension between academic reflection and life-changing involvement. She rightly states that "rational education alone does not heal." I fully agree. If it comes down to the educational process in our schools, I believe that this is the most critical issue. Looking at the western model of academic theological studies I am frustrated. Everyone knows that academia alone does not heal. Everyone is informed about the deficiencies of one-sided academic training in western universities. Nonetheless the whole accreditation business still follows mainly the rational academic path and pushes colleges and seminaries in this direction. On the other hand, new and alternative models of leadership training have been developed. They often tend to move in the opposite direction. Learning by doing, on the job training, learning through involvement, and other concepts attract young people who are tired of university academia. But educators know that involvement, doing, and experience do not automatically lead people to a responsible learning experience. Involvement, doing, and experience need to be complemented by distancing or distanciation, to use Farley terminology, and critical reflection. Some schools have added more and more practical experience and field work to their curriculum but this does not necessarily solve the problem. Too often field education becomes a separated addition to the academic courses with only minimal or no integration with the traditional curriculum. Theory and practice remain separated areas far from an integration of practical involvement and critical reflection. In our European context I can only confess that most theological schools have not yet made significant progress in the integration of theory and practice. There is still a long way to go.

But there are also visions. While I am involved in the above mentioned educational situations, I have also the privilege to do research with the Oxford Centre for Mission Studies. It happens that my topic is the history and the present situation of theological education, especially what can be called the paradigm changes in theological education. In the context of my research I reflect on the discussions in the western world as well as the developments of theological training in the two-thirds world with its challenges to western models of theological training and the experiments of alternative models of ministerial formation. Much has been said and written on theological education. As a community of theological educators we actually know what we ought to do. Looking at the paradigm changes in theological education which have been developing in the last 20 to 40 years several critical areas must be addressed. I will briefly identify five of them:

* The integration of mission into theological studies in such a way that every aspect of theological training becomes a mission-oriented dimension.
* The fragmentation of theological studies as a cumulation of more or less unrelated subjects. This fragmentation calls for an integrative centre which interrelates the different subjects in a meaningful way.
* The problem of 'additionalism', i.e. the strategy to add some new courses or even a new department to the program whenever deficiencies are realised (mission, spirituality, counseling, peace studies, Anabaptist theology). The vision is the integration of such new aspects as dimensions of all courses.
* The institutionalized clerical paradigm which limits theological training to the elite of professional theologians and pastors. The vision is theological training which has the entire people of God in view.
* The problem of the theory-praxis dichotomy which I have referred to earlier. The vision is integrated learning which includes involvement and action as well as critical reflection.

These are my visions.

As we move on with our Bible school and with the project of a new seminary we need such a vision. But I know, the daily struggle for meaningful theological training will be in the space between vision and reality.

CONCLUSION

This final section includes a summary of overall discussion highlights, a brief reference to several issues raised which call for further consideration, and a report on recommendations and projections.

Discussion Highlights

The comprehensive theme of the Consultation—theological education on five continents, within an Anabaptist framework—elicited a number of pertinent considerations both in the plenary sessions and in caucus meetings. Those considerations, including questions, points of clarification and implications, intersect strongly with the two main dimensions of the agenda, that is, the nature and function of theological education, and the significance of having an Anabaptist identity, as registered below.

* There is a tension between vision and reality when it comes to the understanding and the practice of Christian faith within an Anabaptist framework.[1] There is also the question about how much we share with the wider Christian family of faith which should enhance our common theological education endeavors even as we affirm the tenets of Anabaptist identity and practice.

* Theological education must be viewed as a special dimension of the church's broader educational ministry. *Theological education is understood as education for ministry, or for leading and teaching roles. It must be carried out in continuity with*

---

[1] Some Consultation participants called for the establishment of written guidelines on Anabaptist beliefs for consideration of all MWC groups. A number of identifiable "Anabaptist emphases" were highlighted in the course of the meeting, including the following: Jesus Christ is normative in all dimensions of life and faith; the Bible is taken seriously within the church as a hermeneutic community attuned and committed to the reign of God; the church is understood first of all as the believers' church; faith is viewed primarily in terms of discipleship (conformation to Christ in everyday life); it is acknowledged that there is always an inherent church-culture tension which underlies our search for faithfulness and our witness in presence, word and deed; Christian faith calls for a special commitment to peace and justice.

education of all believers for faith and for growth in discipleship, that is, Christian education. The whole educational ministry needs to be affirmed, integrated,[2] renewed and strengthened. Formation and transformation of persons and communities in the light of Jesus Christ—that is, conformation to Jesus Christ—are the guiding principle and the overall purpose in all cases.[3]

* Theological education is especially concerned with training and enabling the leadership (pastors, teachers, evangelists and others) for the sake of the formation of the church in conformity with God's reign. A number of priorities must be consistently followed:

- to identify afresh and work with *Anabaptist perspectives;*
- to educate congregational *teachers* on all levels;
- to enhance theological education opportunities for *women*;
- to allocate more resources on *"non-formal"* ("distance"; "community-based") theological education and to share available resources more widely and wisely;
- to focus on the relationship of theological education to international discussions about partnership in mission.[4]

* Theological education includes teaching and learning for faithful and pertinent theological and ethical discernment. In this

---

[2] In addition to integrating so-called "Christian education" and "theological education," and the overall curriculum as a "balanced diet" of teaching-learning and a comprehensive whole, other dimensions of integration must be considered as well, such as the following: to make education more intergenerational (as an alternative to the fragmentation promoted within the dominant modern culture); and to connect more closely the teaching ministry with other ministries and practices within the life of the church and its witness in society. Further, some Consultation participants underscored the value of much of "secular" education as potentially foundational and/or complementary to theological education; to the extent that that is indeed the case, it points to another area of needed integration.

[3] The need to include personal growth and spiritual formation as a goal of theological education at all levels—especially in formal institutions—is thus explicitly affirmed.

[4] A specific problem identified in connection with this point is that gifted theological educators are often pulled away from the congregation to church institutions and, also frequently, from poorer to richer regions and countries. Such a "brain drain" tends to be associated with the structures of formal education.

Conclusion 129

dimension of theological education, the explicit aim is to articulate our faith convictions (or, our "confession of faith") in a sound and well-grounded way; and that aim includes evaluating and guiding our normative practices (for example as we seek cohesion and integrity in the experience of worship and in the mission endeavors).

Issues for Further Reflection

Together with the affirmations registered in the previous section, a number of pertinent concerns and questions were raised. Those issues calling for further research and dialogue can be summarized under the categories of language, content, and method. In each of those areas, diverse views were expressed, on continuums whose end points are noted below.

* *Language.* The question of the languages we use includes a number of interconnected dimensions that must be carefully addressed:

- communitarian—broader society; the language of our faith communities and the "official language" of the dominant culture,[5] and how they are used in teaching and learning in different congregational, formal and non-formal settings and levels;
- mother tongue—foreign language; the language(s) used in our practices of theological education if other than the mother tongue, including the questions of required translations and the need to affirm the mother tongue over against foreign languages;
- illiterate—literate; the common assumptions of literacy and the challenge of addressing the situation of illiterate persons or groups in our theological education programs (this issue includes the need and opportunity to take fuller advantage of oral materials available everywhere).

---

[5]On this point see Lydia Harder's reference to Walter Brueggemann's notions of "conversation behind the wall" (that is, in the language of the faith community as such) and "on the wall" (that is, in the "foreign tongue" of the dominant culture). Brueggemann himself concludes that the educational ministry of the church must help us all to become truly "bilingual" in the sense of enabling us to carry out simultaneous conversations.

* *Content.*
  - Anabaptist—broader Christian family (and the entire human community); what makes our theological education "Anabaptist" and how our theological education contributes to shape the Anabaptist character of our churches (even as we affirm the commonalities with the larger Christian family) remain as lingering questions in this area[6];
  - Biblically based—life reality grounded theological education; the ongoing challenge of integrating biblical and theological understandings with actual experience,[7] and the related question of appropriate methods of biblical interpretation.

* *Method.* This set of issues must be considered as closely related to those of language and content. Again, several continuums are identified:
  - interactive (participatory, collaborative) methodology—magisterial approach to teaching and learning; the question of creative ways of engaging the learners in the face of a long tradition dominated by the structures of formal education;
  - group specific (men or women/age-group)—heterogeneous, intergenerational; discerning ways to appreciate and utilize the human resources in a variety of settings;
  - theological education for the few—theological education for the many; how to make theological education widely accessible; also, how to realize the vision of education for the whole people of God, on the one hand, and the call to enable the leadership of the church, on the other hand.

---

[6] A number of additional specific questions were raised during the Consultation, including the following: Can a 16th century Anabaptist experience be authentically recovered and appropriated for the 21st century? With which other religious groups do we share a common vision of humanity and of God's life? Does our denominational identity help or hinder the search for a common faith experience? Does the emphasis on the work of the Holy Spirit move us toward a Pentecostal (in contrast to Anabaptist) identity?

[7] This challenge is closely related to the overall question of integrating theory and practice, and also spirituality and academic knowledge, in theological education as a matter of curricular relevance and balance.

Conclusion 131

Recommendations and Projections

The Barrackpore gathering generated rich reflection and dialogue in a very short period of time. During the final session, the Consultation participants unanimously voiced a call for follow up. Several specific recommendations are indicated below.

Make available Consultation materials. This entails editing, publishing, and distributing widely the presentations and responses of the Consultation. It is also hoped that those materials will be translated into French, German, and Spanish and be made available as appropriate.

Encourage research and sharing. This suggestion involves requesting and compiling specific examples, stories, and discussions from member conferences of MWC on how Anabaptist identity is reflected and fostered in different types of theological education programs. Further, the objective is to promote focused study on theological education within an explicitly Anabaptist framework, including the kinds of issues, questions and concerns registered above.

Foster further dialogue and collaboration. It is recommended that MWC consider forming a Theological Education Committee in order to coordinate future activities, and to encourage reflection and conversation, interchange, and cooperation among member conferences. It is also recommended that MWC explore the possibility of initiating a coordinating center to continue networking, to develop a newsletter, and to facilitate sharing theological education resources.

As we pursue these recommendations, to assure that our conversations are honest and comprehensive we will undoubtedly need to keep in focus those diverse points of intersection with theological education which characterize our worldwide Anabaptist family.

Consultation Participants

Héctor Savador Argueta
Guatemala

María Leonor Argueta de Méndez
Guatemala

I.P. Asheervadam
India

Wendy Binks
India

A. Helen Dueck
Canada/Bolivia

Henry W. Dueck
Canada

José Gallardo
Spain

Raúl O. García
Argentina

Lydia M. Harder
Canada

Nancy R. Heisey
USA

Bedru Hussein Muktar
Ethiopia

Mikha Joedhiswara
Indonesia

P. Menno Joel
India

Dickson Keregero
Tanzania

Lawum'etan Kayamba
Congo

Bruce Khumalo
Zimbabwe

Ngombe Kidinda
Congo

John N. Klassen
Germany

Heidi Redier Kreider
USA

Nzash Lumeya
Congo

Emebet Mekonnen
Ethiopia

Albert J. Meyer
USA

Cathy Motuli Mputu
Congo

Handoko Mulyanto
Indonesia

Kinana Mwaku
Congo

Dennis Mweetwa
Zambia

Mteba Ngoya
Congo

Louise Nussbaumer
France

Consultation Participants

Bernhard Ott
Switzerland

R.N. Peter
India

R.P. Vijitha Peter
India

Janet Plenert
Brazil

Steve Plenert
Brazil

Erma Plett
Canada

Stan Plett
Canada

John Powell
USA

Jaime Prieto
Costa Rica

Mary Rao
India

Ravi Sankara Rao
India

G.A. Ineke Reinhold-Scheuerman
The Netherlands

Milka Rindzinski
Uruguay

V.K. Rufus
India

Walter Sawatsky
Canada/USA

Daniel S. Schipani
Argentina/USA

Elvira Schmidt
USA

Henry J. Schmidt
USA

Mbombo Shamwimba
Congo

E.D. Solomon
India

E. Premaleela Solomon
India

Elizabeth Soto-Albrecht
USA

Rafael Stabile
Argentina

Peter Stucky
Colombia

Aristarckhus Sukarto
Indonesia

Siaka Traore
Burkina Faso

Ernesto Wiens
Brazil

Institutions and Programs

Name	Address	Affiliation	Training
AFRICA			
Ethiopia			
Meserte Kristos Bible College	P.O. Box 24227 Addis Ababa	Meserete Kristos Church	Bible School
One Year for Christ Training of Trainers	Meserete Kristos Church P.O. Box 24227 Addis Ababa	Meserete Kristos Church	TEE
Tanzania			
Mennonite Theological College of Eastern Africa	P.O. Box 7 Musoma	Mennonite Churches in Eastern Africa	Bible School
TEE-North Mara Diocese	% KMT Dayoisi ya Mara Kaskazini Private Bag Shirati Hospital Musoma	Kanisa la Mennonite Tanzania	TEE
Congo, D.R.			
Institut Supérieur Théologique de Kinshasa	B.P. 4742 Kinshasa II	AIMM, COM, MBM/S	Seminary
Kalonda Bible Institute	B.P. 18, Tshikapa	AIMM	Bible School
Kikwit Bible Institute School	B.P. 81, Kikwit	CEFMZ, MBM/S	Bible
TEE-Kikwit	% CEFMZ	CEFMZ, MBM/S	TEE
TEE-Kituba	B.P. 4081 Kinshasa II	AIMM	TEE
TEE-Tshiluba	B.P. 18, Tshikapa	AIMM	TEE
Zambia			
Sikalongo Bible Institute	P.O. Box 630131 Choma	BIC	Bible School/ TEE
Zimbabwe			
Ekuphileni Bible Institute	Private Bag M5218 Bulawayo	BIC	Bible School
ASIA			
India			
Mennonite Brethren Bible Institute	Shamshabad via Hyderabad Ranga Reddy Dist. A.P. 509 218	MBM/S	Bible School

Institutions and Programs

TAFTEE Nav Jevan Hospital	Satbarwa Palamav District Bihar	BMM	TEE

Indonesia

Sekolah Alkitab Maranatha	Jalan Brigjen Sudiarto 20 Ungaran, Jawa Tengah	JKI	Seminary
Sekolah Tinggi Agama Kristen Wiyata Wacana	Jl. Diponegoro 33 Pati, Central Java	GITJ	Seminary
Universitas Kristen Duta Wacana	Jalan Dr. Wahidin 5-19 Yogyakarta 55224	GKMI, GITJ, et al.	Seminary/ Secular Studies
Universitas Kristen Satya Wacana	Jalan Diponegoro 52-60 Salatiga 50711	GKMI, GITJ, et al.	Seminary/ Secular Studies

CARIBBEAN, CENTRAL AND SOUTH AMERICA

Argentina

Centro Evangélico de Estudios Biblicos	Mercedes 149 1407 Buenos Aires	Mennonite Churches in Argentina	TEE

Brazil

Centro Evangélico Menonita de teología	R. Venezuela 330 Jardim Nova Europa 13035 Campinas, S.P.	COM, MBM, Mennonite Churches in Brazil	TEE
Instituto e Seminario Bíblico Irmaos Menonitas	Av. Comendador Franco 7770 81560-000 Curitiba - PR	MB	Bible School/ Seminary

Colombia

Seminario Bíblico Menonita	A.A. 53024 Bogotá	COM	Seminary/ TEE

Guatemala

SEMILLA	Apartado 1779 Cd. de Guatemala	Latin American Mennonite Churches	Seminary

Honduras

Mennonite Bible Institute Iglesia Menonita Hondurena	Avenida La República La Ceiba, Atlántida

Paraguay

Centro Evangélico Menonita de Teología Asunción (CEMTA)	C.d.d. 166 Asunción	COM, Mennonite Churches in Brazil, Paraguay and Uruguay	Bible School/ Seminary
Instituto Bíblico Asunción	C.d.c. 1154 Asunción	MBM/S and MB Churches in Paraguay	Bible School
TEE-Asunción	C.d.c. 166, Asunción	EMCC	TEE
TEE-Asunción	C.d.c. 1154, Asunción	MBM/S	TEE

Yalve Sanga Bible School	C.d.c. 984 Asunción	COM, Konferenz der MBG von Paraguay, Vereinigung der MG Von Paraguay	Bible School

Uruguay

Centro de Entrenamiento De los Hermanos Menonitas	Avda. Instrucciones 1695 12400 Montevideo	MBM/S	Bible School
Centro de Estudios y Retiros de las Iglesias Menonitas	3 de Febrero 4381 12900 Montevideo	COM, MBM, Mennonite Churches in Uruguay	Seminary

Venezuela

EMC International Ministries	Apartado 75304 Caracas D.F. 1041-A	EMC	TEE

EUROPE
Germany

Bibelseminar Bonn	Tilsiter Strasse 8 Meckenheim		Seminary

Lithuania

Lithuania Christian College	Malunininku 4 5800 Klaipeda		Liberal Arts

Netherlands

Het Seminarium	Singel 450 NL-1017 AV Amsterdam	ADS	Seminary

Switzerland

Europäische Mennonitische Bibelschule	CH-4410 Liestal	KMS, AEEMF, AMBD MCC, VdM, VDM	Bible School

NORTH AMERICA
Canada

Bethany Bible Institute	Box 160 Hepburn SK S0K 1Z0	MB	Bible School
Canadian Mennonite Bible College	600 Shaftesbury Blvd Winnipeg MB R3P 0M4	GC	Bible School
Columbia Bible College	2940 Clearbrook Rd Clearbrook BC V2T 2Z8	GC, MB	Bible School
Concord College	169 Riverton Ave Winnipeg MB R2L 2E5	MB	Bible School
Conrad Grebel College	Westmount Rd. N Waterloo ON N2L 3G6	GC, MC	Liberal Arts

Institutions and Programs

Institut Biblique Laval	1775 Edouard-Laurin Ville St Laurent PQ H4L 2B9	MB	Bible School
Steinbach Bible College	Box 1420 Steinbach, MB R0A 2A0	EMCC, EMMC Chorititzer, Steinbach Evan. MB Church, Christian Fellowship Church (Mennonite)	Bible School
Toronto Mennonite Theological Centre	47 Queen's Park Cres E Toronto ON M5S 2C3	Inter-Mennonite	Theology

United States

Assoc. Mennonite Biblical Seminary	3003 Benham Ave. Elkhart IN 46517	GC/MC	Seminary
Bethel College	300 E. 27th St. Newton KS 67117	GC	Liberal Arts
Bluffton College	Bluffton OH 45817	GC	Liberal Arts
Eastern Mennonite Seminary	Harrisonburg VA 22801	MC	Seminary
Eastern Mennonite University	Harrisonburg VA 22801	MC	Liberal Arts
Fresno Pacific University	1717 S. Chestnut Ave Fresno CA 93702	MB	Liberal Arts
Goshen College	1700 S. Main St. Goshen IN 46526	MC	Liberal Arts
Hesston College	P.O. Box 3000 Hesston KS 67062	MC	Liberal Arts
Mennonite Brethren Biblical Seminary	4824 E. Butler Ave. Fresno CA 93727	MB	Seminary
Messiah College	Grantham PA 17027	BIC	Liberal Arts
Rosedale Bible Institute	2270 Rosedale Rd Irwin OH 43029	MC	Bible School
Tabor College	400 S. Jefferson Hillsboro KS 67063	MB	Liberal Arts

Note: There are other institutions and programs of theological education where Mennonites and Brethren in Christ work as partners. Mennonite World Conference (8, rue du Fossé des Treize, 67000 Strasbourg, France) welcomes information concerning them to be included in a future update of the present list.

Other Occasional Papers
by the Institute of Mennonite Studies

No.	1	*Biblical Essays on War, Peace and Justice* (out of print)
No.	2	*Theological Education in Missional Perspective* (out of print)
No.	3	*The Bible and Law*
No.	4	*Following Jesus Christ in the World Today* (J. Moltmann) (out of print)
No.	5	*The Pastor-People Partnership: The Call and Recall of Pastors from a Believers' Church Perspective*
No.	6	*Perspectives on the Nurturing of Faith*
No.	7	*Explorations of Systematic Theology* (out of print)
No.	8	*Dialog Sequel to Moltmann's Following Jesus Christ in the World Today*
No.	9	*Essays on War and Peace: Bible and Early Church*
No.	10	*Perspectives on Feminist Hermeneutics*
No.	11	*Essays on Spiritual Bondage and Deliverance*
No	12	*Essays on Peace Theology and Witness*
No.	13	*A Disciple's Christology: Appraisals of Kraus's Jesus Christ Our Lord*
No.	14	*Anabaptist-Mennonite Identities in Ferment*
No.	15	*Alternative Models of Mennonite Pastoral Formation*
No.	16	*Peace Theology and Violence Against Women*
No.	17	*Making Disciples in the Congregation: A guide to Christian formation through the process of mentoring and the experience of congregational worship*
No.	18	*Discipleship in Context: Papers read at the Menno Simons 500 International Symposium, Elspeet, Netherlands, 1996*

To order any of these publications or to receive a complete listing of other IMS publications please contact the Institute of Mennonite Studies, 3003 Benham Avenue, Elkhart, IN 46517-1999; Phone: (219) 296-6239; Fax: (219) 295-0092: E-mail: rliechty@ambs.edu.